LIKE YOU OWN IT

Breakthrough Strategies for Confident Living

CARRIE PERRIEN SMITH

Soar with Eagles

A Publisher Driven
by Vision and Purpose
www.soarhigher.com

*Like You Own It:
Breakthrough Strategies
for Confident Living*

Copyright © 2016 by Carrie Perrien Smith.
All rights reserved.

ISBN-13: 978-0-9834528-7-4
Library of Congress Control Number: 2016900113

No part of this book may be reproduced, stored in a retrieval system, or transmitted in any form or by any means, electronic, mechanical, photocopy, recording, or any other — except for the inclusion of brief quotations in a review — without written permission from Soar with Eagles.

First Edition

Published by
Soar with Eagles
2809 Laurel Crossing Circle
Rogers, AR 72758 USA
www.soarhigher.com

Design and editing by Carrie Perrien Smith

Printed in the United States of America

Dedication

To my husband Tom who
has always encouraged me
to do anything I thought
I was big enough to do.

To my parents Wayne and Phyllis Simpson
who worked hard to give my brother and me
the best foundation for life they could.

To my daughter Darcie who is far more amazing
than she will ever give herself credit for.

To God who continues to amaze me
with what He does through my efforts. Wow!

Contents

Introduction vii

1. Make the First Sale to Yourself 1
2. Become Your Most Amazing You 7
3. Create Your Signature Sixty-Second Commercial 13
   Part 1 of the Sixty-Second Commercial:
   Your Positioning Statement... 14
      The Salesman or Business Owner 14
      The Job Searcher 16
      The Recruiter 17
      The Student 19
   Part 2 of the Sixty-Second Commercial:
   Something That Differentiates You................................ 21
4. Recognize That You Are Already Enough 25
5. Make a Confident First Impression 29
6. Master the Art of Aggressive Friendliness 35
7. Equip Others for Success 41
8. Harness the Power of the Vision Board 45
9. Craft a Strong Personal Brand: Get Their Attention 51
   Your Résumé 53
      Name and Contact Information on Each Page 54
      A Solid Professional Summary.................................... 54
      Specific Skills.. 54
      Achievements... 55
      Employment History 55
      Degrees, Certifications, and Specialty Training........ 55
      Information to Eliminate 56
   Your LinkedIn Profile.. 56
   Professional Photos 57

10. Craft a Strong Personal Brand:
   Build Your Reputation 59
   Platforms for Sharing Content 60
   Writing Content That Positions You As an Expert 63
   Using Social Media to Build an Audience 66
   Spelling, Grammar, and Punctuation Alert 67
   A Word on Social Media Exposure 68
   The World Needs Your Content 68

11. Volunteer to Build Confidence in Your Abilities 69
    Determining Where and How to Volunteer 73
    The Confidence to Accept the Calling 76

12. Make Meaningful Conversation 77

13. Free Your Voice 85

14. Define Your Personal Truth 89
    Eliminating the Negative Self-Talk 92
    Taking the Next Steps for Success 97

15. Lead Well-Organized Face-to-Face Meetings 99
    A Note about Protocol 101
    Planning and Running Productive Meetings 101
    Understanding the Unspoken
    Rules of Meeting Leadership 103
    Using Guest Meeting Organizers 104

16. Step Up and Grab That Microphone 105

17. Look the Part 113

18. Give It All to God 119

19. Soar 125

Introduction

One day it happened. I just got sick to death of people — women and men — leaving their potential on the table because they didn't believe their own worth. I was disgusted at their way they sold themselves short. It didn't matter how much anyone else believed in them or encouraged them; they were never going to amount to anything because they didn't believe they could.

Folks, the first sale you make is to yourself. Until that happens, no one else will buy. You have to believe in your capabilities and your preparation.

I also believe in God, and I see evidence every single day that He loves me and believes in me — in what I am now and what I could be. When we believe in Him and recognize how much He cares about our learning experiences and success, it makes it easier to believe in ourselves and take some risks. Not all my readers believe in God, but my belief in Him makes me who I am.

Since 2002, I've developed techniques to help people network and build business relationships. I weave communication skills into every technique I teach. Hands down, communication is the most important tool in an individual's toolbox.

I've learned over the years that a person's level of confidence in themselves is one of the biggest factors in their success. No matter what their background, if they didn't believe in themselves, they couldn't win in life. This is why I wrote *Like You Own It*. It is loaded with techniques designed to help people to break through their struggles and achieve their fullest potential.

We're all busy today. I wrote concise chapters so you can learn a concept during your break at work, while your baby is napping, before you slip off to sleep at night, or when you find a quiet moment by yourself in the bathroom. It is packed with rock-solid techniques but is short enough to read on a plane trip.

Like You Own It is written for men and women who are ready to break the chains of insecurity, fear, doubt, low self-esteem, and anxiety that prevent them from succeeding.

You don't need anyone else to have confidence in you. You don't need someone or some organization to anoint you "worthy." Do your homework. Believe in your cause or mission. You are ready. You are already enough. Your time is now.

Carrie Perrien Smith
January 2016

1
Make the First Sale to Yourself

One of my favorite things to do is to help people discover their personal genius. Most folks are unaware of what a personal genius might be. It is where they will find their proverbial sweet spot, but first, they must believe it exists. Then they must own it.

Your personal genius is that special capability you have that just comes naturally. You probably didn't go to school to learn it. It would be awesome if you could have taken a test to discover it — like a personality profile test. Some aptitude tests can help you identify it. Sometimes it requires a journey of personal discovery.

I participated in a panel discussion recently at a business club meeting at a private university. I was on the panel with some twenty-something young professionals. They had been in the workforce five years or less, but all held responsible positions. I would have loved to have such responsibility at that phase in my career, some twenty-five years earlier. My perspective was indeed different.

The panel moderator asked each panelist what traits were most highly valued by prospective employers. Each one talked about how students needed to have good strong handshakes and use eye contact and possess calm demeanors. Their intellect and their degrees would take them far as well. Essentially, they suggested that students needed to mold themselves so they would be a great cultural fit for the typical employer.

One panelist described a guy who was so assertive when meeting with potential employers that he was surely scaring them off and ruining his chances of employment. When it came my turn to respond, I wanted to heartily agree with everything they were saying. However, I had to speak some truth that I learned from a couple decades of trying to mold myself into what I thought all employers wanted. Sometimes it wasn't congruent with who I was.

That guy who is assertive? I suggested they hide and watch to see who gets hired first. Assertive Guy's willingness to approach total strangers and ask for the job is a trait that few people master so early in their careers. He would make a great salesman who would serve well the right company.

With his great grade point average and his business degree from a private university, Assertive Guy would easily transition to management within a short time. His strong people skills make him a candidate for a senior management career track.

Assertive Guy probably isn't the best fit for every company. He's probably way too fun for a big accounting firm. His set of skills and bold personality might be over the top for some companies, but he is the perfect fit for the right company.

Should everyone be just like Assertive Guy? Of course not. To act just like him when it isn't authentically you would look obviously incongruent. Can you learn some skills from him? Sure. Borrow some ideas and techniques, but you need to be who you are.

The thing that is beautiful about Assertive Guy is that he already owns who he is, even though some people think he needs to tone it down. The quicker he discovers that his personal genius is his eager, friendly personality and ability to ask for the sale, the sooner he can whittle down the list of potential employers and jobs to pursue.

Should he bypass interviews with companies that he suspects aren't a match for his personal genius? Heck no. At his age or even at mine, interviewing skills are necessary. Each interview provides the opportunity to practice so that he's ready and comfortable with the interviewing process when the right employment opportunity comes along.

The sales profession is a numbers game.
- How many no's does it take to get a yes?
- How many calls does it take to get a meeting with a prospective client?
- How many meetings does it take to get a sale from a prospective client?

When you know what your personal genius is and where it fits in society, it takes fewer no's to get to a yes; it requires a lot fewer calls to get a meeting; and it requires a lot fewer meetings to get a sale.

The lesson that Assertive Guy offers is this: be you and be the most amazing you that you can be. When you are trying to be someone you aren't, you will never expose your authentic self for your prospective employer. I would rather be the real me in an interview than end up in a job for which I'm not a fit. That is a hard truth to embrace when it seems like you are never going to land that next job, but life is too short to spend it doing something that isn't the right fit.

This is why I'm a fan of college students in their freshman or sophomore years networking with people in their chosen industry. College is ridiculously expensive. The sooner students determine whether they are pursuing the right or wrong major, the better. By having a series of conversations with people who work in the field, students may decide to change a major or minor or add some classes to their current degree plan to better prepare them for the workplace.

Way too often, students change majors because they can't cut the college classwork. You can tutor your way through college. It is worth toughing it out if the industry you are training for has jobs that inspire you to run to the office every morning. The best place to get advice about your chosen field is from people who work in your chosen field.

College counselors are the worst place to get education and workforce advice (sorry, counselors!). Most counselors have no idea what is going on in industry. They work in a vacuum! Even the professors are clueless about the world outside the university campus.

Assertive Guy might not end up working in the human resources department for a big legal firm full of suited employees. He has a greater chance of being in charge of corporate training for a company that manufactures fun like Hard Rock Cafe or Walt Disney World.

I hope he'll end up in a place where he can use his personal genius to be the most authentic awesome Assertive Guy that he can be. Most of all, I hope he won't be advised to hide his personality traits just to get the job and end up in a role or a company that he ends up hating. He would find his sweet spot sooner if he is hired for who he is.

Does that mean that we shouldn't pursue professional development? Absolutely not. We need to develop and upgrade skills as time goes along. We need to prepare ourselves for next steps in our lives. That means advancing in a company for some. For others, it means making the big jump into self-employment. When we work to improve ourselves and learn new skills and polish some rough edges, we make sure we are ready for whatever opportunity heads our way.

> "Chase knowledge with reckless abandon."

Professional development is the most efficient way to build your confidence. It comes in different forms. Maybe it is an advanced degree, certification, or training class. You might read books or blogs or watch videos. A mentor or coach can provide personal insight and guidance. Whatever you choose, chase knowledge with reckless abandon.

When you have information that can help others solve problems, it is easy to feel confident in your abilities. We spend too much time trying to *be a confident person*. Instead, we should be working to *feel confident in our abilities*. That is far more attainable.

The first sale you make it to yourself. Until you make that

first sale, no one else buys. We think we can "fake confidence" but we can't. When we try, the only one we fool is ourselves. Our lack of confidence in our own worth is evident by the way we make eye contact, the way we carry ourselves, and in the way we shake hands.

We don't always recognize a lack of confidence, but we feel a sense of incongruence. But when a decision maker determines that you lack confidence, you definitely are not getting the sale.

This is why professional development delivers a fast track to a confident image. When you believe in yourself and the value of your knowledge and ability to serve others, you see your value. In fact, your passion for who you can help is obvious each time you get a chance to talk about it. And when you feel confident and passionate about what you can do, it is easy to feel satisfaction and joy. People will want what you've got.

Seek out your personal genius — the action or character trait at which you excel. If you aren't sure what it is, ask others. You may not get the same answer from everyone, and you may have to work through the responses with a mentor or coach. But prepare to be surprised. I bet you don't know what your personal genius is. The sooner you identify it, the sooner you can bring your most authentic amazing you to whatever you choose to do in life.

2
Become Your Most Amazing You

I spoke to a group of young professionals on the topic of networking for job searchers. The audience members were at a vastly different place than the adult (sometimes older adult) job searchers I talk with about networking. These young people are still trying to fit into a mold and probably won't understand who they really are for years.

I don't think I really understood who I was until I was at least 40 years old. I am a student of every self-development theory there is. I am a sponge. I want to make sure there isn't anything that I don't know.

For the last two decades, maybe longer, I could be characterized as a lifelong learner. It has served me well. It has helped me do my work with excellence. It doesn't mean that everything I attempt turns out excellent, but I bring my best effort to the table.

One attendee asked how to be memorable. It's a valid

question. You want people to remember you when you've met them, right? People don't always have much reason to refer you at the exact moment you meet. Making yourself memorable is a worthy goal.

I liken being memorable to being lucky. It's easy to be lucky when you've prepared your butt off. Being memorable is more about follow up and finding ways to engage with someone periodically than it is delivering a memorable first impression.

Here is the advice I gave the attendees: be the most amazing you there is. When you commit yourself to excellence and being the most amazing you possible, people will pay attention.

Further, God loves our effort to do our best. He wants us to learn through mistakes and success. He wants us to become the most amazing us we can be. I've seen Him take turn my floundering or failing efforts into learning experiences that prepared me for future success. Even though the failure was painful, I learned the most when I searched for the meaning and value in the experience.

We all trip and fall occasionally. Mistakes happen despite proper planning. The world isn't a perfect place. But when we bring our best effort to the project, God catches us when we trip.

Here is an example of what I mean. Decorating isn't my thing. I consider it a necessary evil in my volunteer work. If you have a fund-raiser or event, it is probably going to call for some decorating. For most of what I've done with events, I've been able to delegate decorating.

My Republican women's club had entered our local

Christmas parade during the last months of my term as president. I am a novice when it comes to parade decorating. We entered to give our political candidates a way to get parade exposure. Most couldn't possibly put together their own float or car while dealing with the other demands of a campaign. I just figured we'd carry our banner, put a couple of signs on a car, and have our candidates walk along with us, carry their signs, and hand out candy.

This is probably not news to you but parades usually have a theme. When I was reviewing the parade guidelines more closely, I realized that the organizers expected every entry to follow the theme. I had no idea how I was going to make our little parade entry follow the "Twas the Lights before Christmas" theme.

> "When you commit yourself to excellence and being the most amazing you possible, people will pay attention."

That night, I woke up full of angst. After lying awake in bed worrying about it, I wandered out to the living room and Googled "how to put Christmas lights on your car." The Internet came to my rescue with some tips and tricks. I made a list that included some suction cups and a power converter that plugs into the car lighter. I could then finally go back to sleep.

The beauty of having routines is that you handle day-to-day life on autopilot. That frees you up to focus on these occasional specialty tasks.

Being a task-oriented person, I made my list of items to do. I shopped for ribbon and picked up a power converter and suction cups. My friend reminded me that I had a lighted elephant lawn decoration that would be perfect to add to my Republican parade entry.

On the day of the parade, I washed my car and went through my entire list of parade tasks. I managed to rig the elephant to ride on the back of our convertible Corvette and wrapped a string of lights and some white tulle around the car. We plugged it in to make sure it worked and then headed to the parade site on time.

It wasn't fancy but it followed the parade theme. We weren't there to win awards anyway. We completed any final setup and then left for dinner. Everything had gone perfectly as planned.

We returned from dinner a few minutes before the start time. My husband would drive the parade car, and I would carry the banner with another friend.

My husband gets in and starts the car at five minutes before start time. He looks at me and asks, "Did you know the car is out of gas?"

[Gasp!] Autopilot had failed me. Making sure a car has gasoline is definitely an autopilot task. I was so focused on these parade tasks, I had not noticed the gas gauge on the car. It was on the last tick. It was practically on fumes. The parade route was a couple miles and the car would idle mostly. There was some chance we'd make it.

I talked with our crew and decided it would be best to try to make it to the corner gas station and hope they had empty gas cans to purchase. We were near the end of the parade and wouldn't move for a few extra minutes.

Then something awesome happened. One of the candidates walking with us said he had a gas can in his truck a few yards away. He headed off to get it. I'm thinking he's got an empty can that I can take to the station.

Another crew member watches him return with his can and says, "He's walking like it is full." He is indeed bringing back a full five-gallon can of gasoline. What are the chances that one of our crew would have just bought gasoline for his generator to prepare for winter weather and decided that he'd take it out of his truck the next day instead of that night? SLIM TO NONE!

But that is what happened. He emptied a couple gallons in the car just in time for us to move forward. Parade organizers just shook their heads. This was indeed a miracle.

I worked so hard to prepare and do the best job with our crew's limited capabilities and time to be the most amazing us we could be. This one little detail slipped through the cracks. It would have either sidelined us or gave us the opportunity to push our parade car through the route.

God provided an option that I would never have expected possible. It proved to all of us that God cares about the smallest things. He appreciates when we do our work with excellence and try to do our best. He proved to our little group of believers that He has our back.

That isn't the kind of Christmas miracle that Hallmark movies are made of, but I'll take this real-life Christmas miracle any day of the week. It was a gift from a God who loves us indeed. But when we put forth our very best effort in all we do, He will honor our hard work.

It's easier to be confident when you know that He's got your back.

3
Create Your Signature Sixty-Second Commercial

You've probably heard it called an elevator statement. It is that description with which you can respond when asked on an elevator, "What do you do?" It is brief enough to answer on an elevator ride.

Where I live in Northwest Arkansas, we don't have many multi-story buildings — only a handful of our buildings are more than three floors. The tallest is nine. You'd better have a pretty short elevator statement around here.

That is why I call it a sixty-second commercial. That is a bit more quantifiable. Is it okay if it is shorter? Sure. Can it be longer? Just a little. The idea is to make it concise and specific; not to make the other person's eyes glaze over.

A sixty-second commercial is not intended to be sixty seconds of content you spew when someone asks what you do. Sure, there are some opportunities where you might attend a structured networking group where everyone takes a turn giving their sixty-second commercial.

That isn't nearly as frequent as the opportunity to engage in conversation. Your sixty-second commercial is really sixty seconds of rehearsed and well-structured content that you can weave into a conversation. You want to give someone just enough of it to prompt them to ask, "Really? Tell me more about that."

Your sixty-second commercial is broken into two parts: your positioning statement and something that differentiates you from others like you.

Part 1 of the Sixty-Second Commercial: Your Positioning Statement

There are several ways to approach the positioning statement, depending on who you are and why you are networking. I will cover several options.

The Salesman or Business Owner

A positioning statement formula for someone who is in sales or owns a business looks something like this:

"I'm [your name] and I'm with [your organization's name]. I provide [list the services you provide] so that [the benefit to your client]. A good client for me is [your ideal client]."

Example: SCORE Mentor

"My name is Dana Jones. I'm a volunteer with SCORE. We provide small business mentoring services for free. I work with small business people who want to start or grow their business by improving all aspects of it including profitability, customer service, visibility, and overall success. A great lead for me is someone who is starting a business or has questions about how to make their small business more successful."

Fill in the components of your positioning statement below.

Your name _____

Your organization's name _____

Services you provide _____

_____

_____

Benefit to your client. What results do you provide? What do you love about what you do? _____

_____

_____

Your ideal client _____

_____

_____

Write your own positioning statement here or on another sheet of paper.

_____

_____

_____

_____

_____

_____

The Job Searcher

A positioning statement formula for a job searcher looks something like this:

"I'm [your name] and I'm looking for a [job, opportunity, career change]. I have been working in the [industry] for [length of time] and enjoy [list a few things about your chosen field that inspire you to get up in the morning]. The organizations I've worked with have benefited from my [benefits you provide to your employer]. I'd like my next role to be with a company [with these attributes]."

Example: Information Technology Professional

"My name is Dana Jones and I'm looking for a management position with a local mid-sized company. I have been working in the information technology field for ten years. I've really enjoyed the ability to solve problems with technology and use it to create tools for the user that make their life better. In my last job, I was promoted to supervisor and that really stretched me in my ability to deal with people. I enjoy leading a team and would like to continue developing my skills there. The organizations I've worked with have benefited from my interest in being a student of the field, my work ethic, and creativity. I'd like my next job to be with a manufacturing company because I understand how technology can help the process. I would like to stay in this area because I'm active in some local charities and my family loves it here."

Fill in the components of your positioning statement below.

Your name and the industry you work in _____

_____

The type of role you are interested in _____
_____

Length of time you've worked there _____

What you love about your field _____
_____

Benefit to employers you've worked with _____
_____
_____

The ideal employment situation _____
_____
_____

Write your own positioning statement here or on another sheet of paper.

_____
_____
_____
_____
_____

The Recruiter

A positioning statement formula for a recruiting professional looks something like this:

"I'm [your name and role] and I'm with [your organization's name]. I provide [list the services you provide] so that [the benefit or result you provide]. A good referral for me is [your ideal candidate]."

Example: Information Technology Recruiter

"My name is Dana Jones. I'm a corporate recruiter for a Fortune 500 company. I recruit top talent for our information systems division. I also advise our hiring managers on every step of the recruiting process, from writing their job descriptions to selecting just the right candidate for their team. I love what I do because it prepares both the applicant and the team for a successful future together. I recruit for all our IT jobs, but currently I am searching for a vice president for our information systems audit division. A good referral for me is a candidate with at least five years of related experience plus three or more years of experience as a supervising manager. The ideal candidate is someone with auditing experience within the consumer products, manufacturing, service, or public accounting technology auditing industries."

Fill in the components of your positioning statement below.

Your name and role _____

_____

Your organization name _____

Services you provide _____

_____

Benefit and results you provide to your hiring managers and applicants. Why do you love what you do? _____

_____

_____

Your ideal candidate _____

_____

_____

_____

Write your own positioning statement here or on another sheet of paper.

_____

_____

_____

_____

_____

_____

The Student

This one is easy to adapt based on the age of the student. A positioning statement formula for a student looks something like this:

"I'm [your name] and I'm in [your grade in school]. I go to school at [school name] in [the city it's in]. My favorite class is [class]. I enjoy it because [why you enjoy it]. When I grow up, I want to be a [career position] because [why you'd like to do that job]. In my free time, I enjoy [what you enjoy doing]. My favorite activity to do with my family is [the activity]."

Example: Fifth-grade Student

"My name is David Jones, and I'm in fifth grade. I go to

Lingle Middle School in Rogers. My favorite class is PE because I enjoy playing the different games. I also like that we never have homework. My other classes have enough of that. When I grow up, I'd like to be a coach that works for the Dallas Cowboys. They are my favorite team, and it would be fun to meet all the players. In my free time, I watch sports and play video games. My favorite thing to do with my family is getting together with my cousins after church on Sunday."

Fill in the information below to write your positioning statement.

    Your name _____

    What grade you're in _____

    Where you go to school and what city it's in _____

    _____

    Your favorite classes and the reason they are your favorites _____

    _____

    _____

    What you'd like to be when you grow up and why ____

    _____

    _____

    What you enjoy doing in your free time _____

    _____

    Your favorite activity with your family _____

    _____

    _____

Write your own positioning statement here or on another sheet of paper.

_____

_____

_____

_____

_____

_____

Part 2 of the Sixty-Second Commercial: Something That Differentiates You

Regardless of what you do, you are in sales. Salespeople who can differentiate themselves will almost always win the prize. When you look for something that makes you a better choice than your competitors — that differentiates you — think of key skills or talents that your competitors don't offer. Think of something that will make your potential employer's or client's life so wonderful that they have to know more.

Some people use this portion of their sixty-second commercial to share knowledge about their field. That helps position them as an expert. In tough times or good, an expert with up-to-date knowledge has an advantage.

In the case of meeting someone who works inside your company (such as a senior manager), this section can be adapted to explain the value of your skills and services to your hiring managers and senior managers. This can position you as an expert and a valued partner.

List all the things that differentiate you — skills or talents the others don't have.

_____

_____

_____

The other person is tuned into WIIFM (what's in it for me). How can you make your client's or potential employer's life better?

_____

_____

What industry knowledge can you share that would demonstrate you are an expert in your field? If you are using this in an interview, you should consider adding why you think you'd like to work for that company or client (this requires researching the company before the interview). _____

_____

_____

_____

Write your statement about what differentiates you from your competitors here or on another sheet of paper. Without mentioning anything about your competitors or others like you, develop a statement from the information above that will build on your positioning statement.

_____

_____

_____

_____

Practice, Practice, Practice!
Revise and Refine as Needed

Use your sixty-second commercial every chance you get. Practice will make it seem much more natural. Get comfortable enough with it to worry less about what you are going to say and instead concentrate on the reactions to your sixty-second commercial. It should make people want to know more by inspiring them to ask questions. If they look confused after listening to your sixty-second commercial, you should consider refining it.

When time permits, begin by engaging the other person in some meaningful conversation to gauge what you need to tell him. Borrow a secret from successful salespeople: spend more time asking educated questions about the other person than you do talking. The other person is more receptive if he knows you understand his needs and interests.

If you have time to prepare before the meeting, in the case of a job interview or business meeting, do some research on the company. Arrive with a list of questions. Coming prepared to create meaningful conversation will show that you value the person's time and demonstrate your good communication and people skills. It can also help you determine the next step with this person. In the case of a job interview or sales call, the questions can help you understand whether this is the right company or client for you.

4
Recognize That You Are Already Enough

It is surprising how many people don't realize how important their ideas are — and how important *they* are. They think they need to get one more degree. They are waiting for someone to recognize them as an expert. That is simply not necessary in most cases.

Changing the world is not rocket science or brain surgery. Those occupations require specific educational degrees and certifications. The qualifications for everything else are in your hands.

What you need is the ability to recognize needs. What problems that need solutions sit right under our noses? I've worked in communications and marketing for many years. The whole idea of marketing is to put a solution on your radar for a problem you didn't know you had. Just because society hasn't deemed something a problem, it doesn't mean that it isn't a problem. Right?

During the 2015 Arkansas legislative session, one well-meaning legislator presented a bill to do away with Daylight Savings Time. That was a clear sign that legislators had run out of meaningful bills to present. It failed miserably, not because people like changing their body clocks twice a year. It failed because no one thought it was a problem worthy of an important process. The problem should be worthy of the work needed to design a solution.

You also need a natural curiosity — the ability to wonder how the situation could be improved. You need to be willing to look past the filters that color our perceptions to see the causes and truth in the gray areas. You need to ask questions until you unearth the causes and possible solutions. You need to ask "why" and "how" many times to many people.

The thing about asking questions is that you can ask them in a way that skews the responses toward any outcome you want. If you are truly curious, you will look at the situation with the innocence of a child. No hidden agenda — just a willingness to explore every nook and cranny. You must expect to be surprised by your findings. If you are not surprised along the journey, you have not asked enough questions of enough people.

You need initiative — a heaping helping of it. Don't wait for someone to agree there is a problem. Don't wait for someone to deem you worthy of solving the problem. And please, please, please don't wait for someone to step forward to help just because you share a graphic on Facebook that makes a snarky comment about the need. One hundred people posting comments on a Facebook graphic doesn't equate to initiative. All that is make you look like a complainer.

If it is a problem worthy of your concern, it is worthy of a solution. You can start a movement all by yourself, but it first requires you to take initiative.

Finally, you need to share your vision for solving the problem. Pray about it. Tell the story about how the problem captured your attention and tugged at your heart. As you walk the journey of exploring the causes, talk about what you saw with your own eyes. Tell the stories of the people who deal with the problem. Share your ideas about solving the problem so people can play devil's advocate and springboard off of the ideas.

The more you are willing to be vulnerable, the better your solution to the problem will be. And it is okay to be wrong, especially if it ultimately means a better solution will emerge. Making mistakes and being wrong is part of the journey to the best possible solution.

Here's how it looks in real life.

> "You need initiative — a heaping helping of it."

My friend Kay Scott grew up in a restaurant family. Woven into her young life were the moments and challenges of running a local Italian restaurant. The recipes were hand-crafted from pure ingredients in their modest kitchen.

Kay grew up with an understanding of how to put a meal on the table for her family. She began to volunteer for a facility that provided transitional living accommodations. They bridged the gap between a battered women's shelter and government-subsidized housing. The facility provided structure and mentoring that didn't exist in the lives of many of the residents and their children.

At first, she didn't know what her real calling was in her volunteer work at the facility. Then one day, she realized that the fresh meat, fruits, and vegetables were rotting in the refrigerator. Puzzled, she asked how this could happen. This was high-quality food.

What she found was that the residents didn't know how to prepare it. Many had grown up on government assistance programs in households where no one cooked. Food came in a box that you opened and popped into the oven. The only other affordable food was passed across the counter of a fast-food restaurant.

Kay created a series of classes that met the residents where they were at — in transition to a better life and willing to learn. She taught them how to cook with five spices and whatever fresh ingredients they had on hand. Parents and kids learned, for the first time in many cases, how to properly prepare a nutritious meal for their family.

And along the way, as people cleaned and chopped and cooked, they had conversations about meaningful topics and made memories that will last a lifetime.

You can do that too. You are already enough.

Make a Confident First Impression

You are about to walk into a meeting with a potential client. If you sell this deal, it will be the injection of cash flow that your fledgling company needs. You are excited and freaked out all at the same time.

Or maybe it is a job interview or the first time at a new networking group or a blind date. There are as many reasons to rock a confident first impression as there are reasons to make you scream on the inside.

Here are eight tips for making a confident first impression. You are not going to believe how easy this is.

The first tip is to smile. I'm not talking about a grin like the Cheshire cat in *Alice in Wonderland*. Give a warm, engaging, and relaxed smile.

This is a great tip for meeting someone new, but I've found it comes in handy when I run into someone I haven't seen in a long time. I find I get a little hung up on how I might have changed since they saw me last. You know — graying hair or pounds gained or lost.

I discovered that a warm smile as we chat keeps their eyes connected to mine so I feel I've reduced the chance they'll notice anything negative. I try to tell myself that people don't notice things like that because I personally don't. However, we all know too many people who comment on how much someone has aged since they last saw them. When you are working hard to make a confident first impression, you sure don't need to worry about something silly like that. That simple smile will cover it all.

And that leads me to my second tip: make eye contact. Eye contact in America means trustworthiness and respect. That doesn't mean you want to leer at someone or stare too long. You simply want to make eye contact as often as possible.

There are three types of learner/communicators: visual, kinesthetic, and auditory. Visual people gather information from what they see. Kinesthetic people gather information from what they feel or experience. The auditory people gather information from what they hear.

Let's talk for a moment about eye contact and the auditory learner/communicator. You'll often find that technical and analytical people lean toward being auditory. Perhaps you've noticed them looking down when you talk with them. They mean no disrespect when they do this.

Actually, it means they are concentrating closely on what you are saying. The auditory learner/communicator finds himself distracted by other stimuli when listening. When they are looking down, it blocks out some of the other distractions such as facial expressions and surrounding visual interruptions. This allows them to gather meaning more easily from your words, emotion, and vocal inflection.

You may be one of those auditory people, and that is why you find it terribly distracting to make eye contact during a conversation. Keep working at it though because most people don't realize looking away is a coping mechanism for you. Make eye contact as often as possible.

My third tip for making a confident first impression is to get an attitude — and I'm not talking about your teenage daughter's attitude. I'm talking about a winning attitude.

Humans are wired to connect. We are drawn to people who have positive attitudes. You've met them. They are the ones who are grateful for the lessons in life's challenges. They embrace the good times and muster up the strength to weather the hardest times. The worst nod they give to their hardest days is to describe them as "tough." They find ways to win despite it all.

Life deals us hard days. Sometimes we have hard weeks. Heck, we even get hard years. But the person we are drawn to is the winner who makes the best out of it all. It is indeed the secret to being attractive (some pun intended).

If you want to make a confident first impression, follow my fourth tip and extend a firm, full-palm handshake. People judge us by our handshake. Is it strong, too hard, clammy, or limp? A weird handshake can distract someone from hearing a single word you say.

If you want an honest opinion about your handshake, ask your broccoli friend. That's what my friend Tom calls that person we have in our life who will tell us, without hesitation, that we have broccoli in our teeth. Find out if you have a distracting handshake and fix it.

The women's liberation movement has created a lot of questions for men. One of those questions arises when it comes time to shake hands. Do they extend their hand first? Do they wait to see if the woman extends her hand? Even women aren't sure whether to shake another woman's hand. So many uncertainties.

Ladies, be the first to extend the handshake. In America, a handshake still means business.

Tip number five for making a confident first impression is to stand tall. Your clothes hang nicer. You breathe easier too, and that is always welcome when you are meeting someone new.

And speaking of clothes, my sixth tip is to dress so that you feel confident. That may mean dressing the same as everyone else at an event or a couple of steps better. It is an individual choice, but choose the option that will make you feel so good that it will take your mind off what you are wearing.

It is so easy to drag around a head full of negative self-talk. Dressing properly is a great way to eliminate some of the distractions that keep you from feeling confident.

If you are unclear about the dress code at an event, call ahead. If you are speaking to a group, dress a notch or two better than the audience. If you are attending a chamber of commerce networking mixer and your usual business uniform is slacks and a shirt with your name on it, wear it. It is part of your brand. Just make sure whatever you choose is clean, flattering, and impeccably pressed.

Sure, clothes are important but nothing looks better on you than tip number seven: a fine set of manners. I'm not talking about being stuffy and proper. I'm suggesting that you be gracious and kind. That means sometimes overlooking someone else's bad manners.

Finally, my eighth tip for making a confident first impression is to look organized. This is a huge challenge for me because I often find myself with multiple appointments back to back. I finish one project what seems like seconds before the next one begins, and I don't have time to put everything away from the first project. Never mind all the times I juggle multiple projects and get interrupted before I get all the moving pieces tucked neatly into their folders.

You may know where everything is in your horizontal filing system (also known as the stacks on your desk). You may have just rushed in from appointments and errands, and you have loose papers hanging out of your planner. These little missteps are causing people to make critical judgments about you. It isn't fair and it isn't right, but it happens.

> "Ladies, be the first to extend the handshake. In America, a handshake still means business."

Do what you can to look organized so you don't miss the chance at a referral to new client or job opportunity. Take a minute to check your purse or planner to make sure it is zipped. If it's overstuffed, take a few minutes to organize it and remove unnecessary items. I often take a bulky item or two out of my purse before I get out of the car to go into a meeting just so my purse looks neat.

If you struggle with your office neatness, schedule a day to sort through your stacks and purge or file those items. If your office organization project requires professional intervention, make the investment. Your future could depend on it.

There you go — eight super-easy tips for making a confident first impression. You've got this. You're going to be awesome!

6
Master the Art of Aggressive Friendliness

Come with me and be a fly on the wall. I walk in the building where a networking event is just beginning. The entrance is washed in autumn sunshine. The loud chatter of voices echoes throughout the building. I've attended this particular networking group at least a hundred times over the years. There is casual networking time during check in, followed by announcements once we settle into our chairs. Food is served, and then we have more structured networking activities.

My time is limited and God made me an introvert, so I need a plan to make the most of this networking event. For years, I've set my goal to meet five new people before I begin to visit with people I already know.

That goal has served me well. It is natural to gravitate to people you already know when you attend an event with a room full of people. First time or hundredth time, you still get nervous. Being one of those task-oriented introverts, being armed with a goal gives me a checklist. That always brings an introvert comfort.

I like to start accomplishing my goal of meeting five new people while I'm checking in. At this particular networking event, about thirty percent are first-time attendees. I don't attend every meeting, so there are a number of people who I don't recognize from previous meetings. It is usually easy to get into line next to someone I don't know.

If I do know the people in line, I might fiddle with my purse or business cards or phone for a minute or two so I can wait for someone new to get in line. Then I fall in line behind them.

It's time to get the attention of the person next to me in line. I wait for a minute to see if she is going to initiate the conversation, but she is avoiding eye contact. It's like we're on an elevator, and she is waiting for the doors to open. At this event, walking up to the check-in table where someone greets you and checks your name off the list is equivalent to the elevator door opening.

I try to make eye contact and introduce myself, "Hi! I'm Carrie Smith. Is this your first time here?" She turns toward me, nods, and says, "Yes." Then, she looks back toward the check-in table, waiting for her elevator exit. She has six people in line in front of her. She's not going anywhere.

I say, "Welcome. You're going to enjoy this. You are among friends. There are lots of new people each month." I explain what usually happens so she'll know what to expect.

Then I ask, "What do you do?" I use the questions from my Meaningful Conversation Template to lead the conversation (see Chapter 12: Make Meaningful Conversation). That task-oriented introvert in me likes having a tried-and-true template but there is more to having a prepared set of questions than that.

The prepared questions allow me to plan what I'm going to ask next so I can focus on what the other person is saying. That addresses the real discomfort in meeting someone new, doesn't it? We are so worried about what we are going to say next that we can't concentrate on what the other person says.

> **The prepared questions allow me to plan what I'm going to ask next so I can focus on what the other person is saying.**

Using the Meaningful Conversation Template puts me in the driver's seat of the conversation. By taking responsibility for leading that conversation, it also puts the other person at ease because she doesn't have to worry about what she will say next. It honors her by placing her at the center of the conversation. She more likely to remember me later because I made her feel valued and interesting. Her anxiety-driven, self-conscious, negative self-talk disengages for a few minutes while I ask her about what she does, what her company does, and what she enjoys doing outside of work.

As we get near the front of the line, I say, "I'm glad we met. Do you have a business card?" She may or may not have told me her name at this point. When you are nervous about doing something new, you forget a small detail like that.

I look at the card and close the conversation, "Jill, you are going to really enjoy today. It was nice chatting with you."

She turns to talk with the person at the check in table. The figurative elevator door just opened, and she walks out.

Once I check in, I move on to meet my next four people. I'm free to chat briefly with people I already know after that goal is met. I don't linger too long though. There are more people to meet. I can schedule a coffee meeting or a phone call for a more in-depth conversation.

And since lunch is part of this networking event, I wait to sit down, scoping out a table where I don't know everyone. Once the formal networking begins, I'll have the opportunity to meet even more new people that way.

The kind of meaningful conversation I've just explained lasts about six or seven minutes. The person I meet may not ever turn the conversation around and ask about me, and that's okay. I found plenty of reasons to follow up during our conversation.

People don't usually do business with us or refer us based on a single conversation. Dropping someone an e-mail or handwritten note is a great way to follow up. You might follow up with a phone call (be sure to leave a voice mail if the person isn't available). I suggest you set up a time to get together for coffee as often as you can. Those frequent conversations are where lifelong business relationships are forged.

I love taking responsibility for leading the conversation because I get precisely the information I need to prepare for the next conversation. It also helps me determine when or if there should be a next conversation.

Here is a warning though: you may meet someone and think, "I don't think he will ever do business with me or even know my typical customer." Never, ever assume that a person won't be worth a follow up based on those criteria. You would be surprised who people know.

And just because they don't know anyone now, it doesn't mean they won't meet someone you need to know. I have had many conversations where someone told me they were looking for someone or something in particular — a client, a job, a potential employee, or a service provider — but I didn't know anyone who fit that description. Within a few days though, I would meet exactly that type of individual or hear about an opportunity that was a great match.

When you embrace the risk to go out and meet new people, God uses you to connect others. No matter what your faith walk is, we can agree that serving something bigger than ourselves is worth the risk of feeling uncomfortable. Connecting others is a high calling. Plus, being that person who is a known connector makes us more memorable.

It helps me maintain top-of-mind awareness with those I meet so that when they meet my ideal client, they remember me. If I built that relationship right, they can probably tell my story with more credibility than I can. A referral from someone else is far more powerful than me reciting my sixty-second commercial. There is a time and place for giving a sixty-second commercial, but weaving that content into a series of conversations cements you in their minds.

You've heard the saying, "People don't care how much you know until they know how much you care." The meaningful conversation is where you prove how much you care.

7
Equip Others for Success

This commentary has been stirring in me for awhile. Too many of the people I admire are enamored with idea of empowering people — like they are doing something incredibly powerful with the act of empowerment.

I want to step lightly here because I don't want to crush anyone's spirit. When someone finds an idea they love — one that they would die for on a mountain in the wilderness — it is wrong for someone to stomp all over it with their well-intentioned commentary. I didn't want to be the stomper.

My desire is to urge these empowerers to take the more risky next step. I want to say it in a way so they would hear the positive intent in my message.

But it has to be said: empowerment is playing small.

Empowerment isn't the beginning or end of the journey. It might put a spark in someone's mind that might — MIGHT — inspire someone to initiate a journey. But the truth is that it will never really guarantee that you are helping someone become all she could be — all she was *created to be*.

Empowerment is just one step ahead of encouragement. This illustrates the difference.

> **Encouraging:** Come on, little buddy. Let's go see if you can go potty.
>
> **Empowering:** Go ahead, little buddy. You can go to the bathroom by yourself.

See? It's playing small. Empowerment is little more than a trite inspirational saying made into a graphic to post on Facebook or a plaque for your wall.

You have way more to offer than that. If you really want to serve something bigger than yourself, don't stop at *empowerment*. Move along to *equipping someone*.

Daring to take a challenge to equip someone means getting your hands dirty. Walk along the hard road with him. Encourage him when necessary. Recognize his personal genius and help him see it too. Believe he can do it. Hold him accountable. Help him recover when he stumbles. Be courageous so he can see what it looks like. Set the example.

You don't have to be very far ahead yourself to reach back and bring someone along behind you. As you learn and make mistakes, someone else can benefit by watching and learning from your process. If you think that sounds a lot like mentoring, you are correct. Equipping is a close relative of mentoring.

I'm a fan of mentoring. I am convinced that the mentor learns far more from the process than the mentee. Working with someone teaches us to communicate better. We learn to ask better questions to help the mentee discover the answers she has inside herself. We give more exact, careful feedback. Our responses become more thoughtful and planned. And when we mess it all up by saying the wrong thing — or the right thing the wrong way — we learn how to straighten it out.

So you are probably wondering how mentoring and equipping others will help you to be more confident, right?

Well, as you work to help someone else, you place the focus on them. We spend a lot of time worrying about how we look to others. Being inwardly focused is the enemy to confidence. It creates an environment where negative self-talk and doubt festers. The truth is that other people aren't really thinking that much about what we look like and do.

But what about those people who pontificate about every irritating person and pet peeve on Facebook? Those who are busy sitting behind a computer posting criticisms about others on Facebook do little to help anyone else. They are simply stirring the pot and distracting the rest of us from using our time and energy in a beneficial way.

The world needs more people who are willing to use their skills and talents to lift up someone else. It is the greatest reward for your efforts as a mentor and equipper when your mentees are ready to move on past you to the next step in their life. There might be no higher calling than to prepare people for their next step. When we help other people become more successful, we recognize that we have much to offer.

Who is in charge of the mentoring relationship — the mentor or the mentee? The mentee should drive the relationship. You may see greatness in someone but until they choose to see it and develop it, they will never use it to move themselves forward.

This is why the mentee's initiative is crucial. There are too many great people who want your help to waste it investing in a person who doesn't want to advance. Feel free to encourage someone and let her know you are always willing to help, but save your best mentoring for a mentee who wants to be equipped. When she is ready, she will drive the relationship.

Keep in mind that you are often mentoring people from a distance. I've learned a great deal from others — their mistakes, their successes, and their responses to life's challenges and questions. We never exchanged the "M" word and maybe they never knew they were mentoring me from a distance. They might never even know who I am.

The power of this whole idea of being mentored from a distance is this: you might be unaware someone is learning from your actions. That should scare the hell out of you just as much as it proves that every action you take matters.

You might have heard someone define integrity as doing the right thing when no one is looking. As a woman of faith, I know at the bare minimum, God is looking. But there is every chance that others are looking too, even if I think my most insignificant action seems unimportant. I now recognize that I am possibly modeling the way for someone else.

Go ahead. Reach back, grab someone's hand, and bring them along behind you. You have much to offer someone else.

8
Harness the Power of the Vision Board

I've been a big goal-setter since my early 20s. I've seen the evidence that putting plans on paper sets the wheels in motion. Even goals that I thought were unreachable due to uncontrollable circumstance somehow happened on time. When you write goals down and review them every day, they become reality.

The vision board (sometimes called a dream board) works much the same way. Basically, you clip a few photos or words from magazines that represent your goals and what you want your life to look like. Then you affix them to a board and hang it on the wall in a place where you can look at it every day.

Admittedly, I was a slow convert to the vision board process. I was an artist and trained to be a technical illustrator. I spent my career hours converting theory and two-dimensional drawings into three-dimensional visuals. I didn't need someone to draw me a picture to visualize the outcome. My goals written on paper worked for me just fine.

But there is an important lesson here for us: just because I don't need it doesn't mean others don't need or want it.

I eventually realized that many people benefit from using a vision board. They need that visual every day to keep them working toward their goals. When those visuals are tied to written goals, the images remind them of the goal and the timeline attached to it. Using a tool to help us visualize our goals and our future enhances and improves the goal achievement process.

When you meet goals, you build confidence. You feel more successful. Using a vision board helps you accomplish more.

How to Get Started

You need a piece of poster board, scissors, and a glue stick. Feel free to use a cork board with push pins. Veteran vision board users update their images periodically. A cork board can offer you some flexibility. You can also use a smart phone application or put digital images together in a photo-editing software application. Whatever you choose, make sure it is easy to view on a daily basis.

You also need some photos. Words are okay to use too. You can print these photos from images on the Internet. Magazines are a great resource.

Use these ideas for image elements for your vision board:

- **Relationships.** If you are married, include a photo of you and your spouse enjoying life. If you are single and looking, put a photo that resembles someone you would like to spend your life with. Be even more specific about what this life mate does for fun or work. How many children do you want? Are they natural or adopted or foster children? Use photos to represent that.

- Extended family. Who do you want to spend your time with? Add pictures of siblings, children, grandchildren, parents, and friends. If you don't have a lot of friends but want more, clip pictures of what type of people they might be. Do they work in your same profession? Are they in the same place in life you are (single, young married couple, or divorced with children, for example)? What kind of activities do you enjoy together?

- Home. What kind of place would you like to call home? Is it a city apartment, country home, or suburban home? Is it decorated in a traditional style or is it more contemporary?

- Location. If you could live anywhere, where would it be? Is it another city or state or country? Is it rural or urban or something in between? Maybe your dream is to reduce your life to a small footprint and live off the grid in a tiny house. If you love the city where you live, be sure to include that on the vision board.

- Cars or recreational vehicles. What is your daily driver? Do you have a dream car? Do you imagine yourself tooling around town on a Segway? Maybe you imagine seeing the country in an RV. Maybe your family enjoys water sports. Include those types of vehicles too.

- Vacations. Do you have dream vacations you've always

> "Using a tool to help us visualize our goals and our future enhances and improves the goal achievement process."

wanted to take? Or is your perfect vacation a weekend trip to the woods? Do you vacation with family, friends, or alone?

- Hobbies. Are there places you'd like hang out more often (the book store or coffee shop, for instance)? Do you have current hobbies you can't imagine life without? Would you like to start a new hobby like knitting or horseback riding? Is your hobby time spent with others or alone? Who would you like to spend it with?

- Pets. Do you want pets? What kind of pet would you like to have? Do you imagine your life with a dog, cat, guinea pig, or fish? Is your pet a purebred or a mixed breed rescued from an animal shelter? What does your pet look like?

- Career. Is there a new position or career achievement you'd like to attain? Do you see yourself self-employed? Do you work at home or in a high-rise tower? Is there a college degree you want? What type of job do you want?

- Volunteer activities. Is there an organization or activity that serves a cause you are passionate about? Do you volunteer there now or would you like to start? What does the organization do and who do they serve? Is it in your city or on the other side of the world? What would you like to do — raise money, plan events, or make phone calls?

- Words or quotes that keep you going. Find quotes that fit where you are going or where you find wisdom or peace. Seek out quotes that are all one piece or piece them together with a collection of words. You can also cut and paste quotes from the Internet into a Microsoft Word document and play with different fonts, colors, and sizes to add a creative flair to your vision board.

- **Emotions.** Remember this important element. A satisfying life isn't about accumulating things. Things can help you enjoy life, but how you feel is more important. Do you want to be happy, challenged, or in love? Really reflect on the emotions you feel throughout the day. When do you feel the very best?

There are plenty of ideas to get you started. Remember that there are no rules. Your vision board should look like the life you imagine living, but be sure to include elements of the life you have now.

And you aren't the only one who needs a vision board. This would be a fun activity with friends. Have each one show up with a handful of magazines, open a bottle of wine, and put on some music. This isn't to say that it couldn't be an intimate experience alone or with your spouse or immediate family members. However, you'll get more ideas that you hadn't thought of when you have more people sharing ideas.

Give it a try and watch how different your life will look in a year.

9
Craft a Strong Personal Brand: Get Their Attention

We are barraged with thousands of marketing messages on a daily basis. As a longtime student of marketing strategy, I have learned to adapt those concepts to help individuals build their personal brand. I work mostly with professional speakers, authors, and political candidates, but these work for anyone.

We all have a personal brand. You may not realize it, but people look at you and see a certain set of qualities. You can choose to mold your personal brand or just let it happen. I beg you to mold it.

While a carefully crafted personal brand is necessary for professional or political reasons, everyone can reap benefits from a strong brand image. By being intentional about your personal brand, you influence what people believe about you.

Of course, you have to buy in to those beliefs about yourself first. I give you the technique for doing just that in Chapter 14: Define Your Personal Truth.

When you craft your personal brand, you should highlight attributes that increase demand for you and your skills. The process is a big confidence builder. Seeing your experience and your expertise in a concrete format drives home your value.

While I love the attention-getting elements, they usually won't provide you the opportunity to expose the reputation-building elements of your personal brand like your ideas, intellect, and integrity. That is why I love to see people use content-writing and sharing tools like blogging and social media to enhance their brand. I'll talk more about the reputation-building elements of your personal brand in the next chapter.

The attention-getting elements of a personal brand are those that provide evidence of hard skills such as achievements and roles you've held. Résumés and LinkedIn are currently the most commonly used tools for showcasing the attention-getting elements of your personal brand.

I also include photos in this category. Even though photos are not included on a résumé, everyone should include a photo on their LinkedIn profile.

Everyone should update their résumé and LinkedIn profile at least once a year. It provides you a chance to review your achievements and refresh the attention-getting elements of your personal brand. You should update your profile photos regularly as well.

Now I'll walk you through the attention-getting elements and tell you how to get the most out of them.

Your Résumé

For many who rely on employment with a company, the résumé is the gold standard for personal branding. It needs to look clean and concise and include key words used in your industry. Today's résumé information needs to flow seamlessly into a digital format that allows search engines to compare résumé key words to job descriptions.

A human will review your résumé eventually so it needs to look well organized and pleasing to the eye. However, you are also designing your résumé to scan cleanly into an electronic filing system. Stick to simple fonts like Times and Arial, and avoid text smaller than 8 point (10 or 11 point is better). Avoid overformatting your text. Stick to bold, but use it only when necessary.

> "Today's résumé information needs to flow seamlessly into a digital format that allows search engines to compare résumé key words to job descriptions."

Formatting doesn't usually present a problem when you are uploading a digital file. However, underlining or italicizing text can trip up the scanning software.

There are many different views about content in résumés. Here is what I've learned you need to include if you want to get someone's attention.

Name and Contact Information on Each Page

Make your name and contact info the heading on page one. Put a smaller version of it in the footer on the subsequent pages. This ensures someone can piece your résumé back together should the printed pages get separated.

Contact information should include the name you usually go by, your personal phone number, personal mailing address, and a professional-sounding e-mail address (get a new one if yours is like dragonslayer83@yahoo.com).

A Solid Professional Summary

Your professional summary will resemble your positioning statement I talked about in Chapter 3: Create Your Signature Sixty-Second Commercial. That is a good template to use for crafting the professional summary.

Do not include this text anywhere in it: "I'm seeking a job that utilizes my skills." They will not read further and you will not get the job.

Take the time to write a professional summary that accurately describes who you are and the value you will bring to your employer.

Specific Skills

If specialty software knowledge is crucial to your job, mention it. Include hard skills and soft skills. Technical jobs should emphasize hard skills such as analysis or program coding. Management-level jobs should emphasize soft skills such as motivating teams, developing others, and leading projects and groups. Some jobs such as nursing or massage therapy will mention both soft and hard skills because of the nature of the care they provide.

Craft your skill list to the industry you want to work in. If you are new to the industry or just getting out of college and don't know what is considered important, meet with people who currently work in the industry to get some ideas.

Achievements

Your achievements section needs to be concise and specific. Find the "what's in it for the company" angle. What is the benefit to the employer? It is appropriate to mention being Employee of the Month, but your potential employer wants to know how you contributed to the bottom line.

Also try to find opportunities to talk about how you worked with teams to accomplish big tasks or how you mentored others. That will score big in the people skills category.

Employment History

When listing your employment history, include the company name, city, state, and years you worked there. Also include the position you held.

You may decide to list your specific achievements with each job. It just depends on the types of roles you've held. When someone builds a career over twenty years in a single industry doing similar roles, her résumé will look a little different than the résumé for someone who is beginning a career and mentioning previous part-time jobs.

Degrees, Certifications, and Specialty Training

The final section is the list of major degrees and certifications.

Don't list the minor ones unless they make you more qualified for the position you want (such as a commercial driver's license).

It's okay to include the dates. Don't worry about exposing your age. You don't know if a hiring supervisor is going to lean toward more mature or prefer newly minted.

If you are applying for a position with a company that might discriminate against you for any reason, you'd be better off to get weeded out earlier. Life is too short to work for that type of employer.

Information to Eliminate

Don't include a photo on your résumé. You don't need to list hobbies and personal interests (unless they reinforce the experience and expertise needed for the job for which you are applying). Skip the note stating that references are available upon request. That is understood, and including it wastes valuable space.

Your LinkedIn Profile

The information on your LinkedIn profile will transfer nicely from your résumé. If you don't need a résumé for your career, you definitely need a LinkedIn profile. Recruiters use it heavily but so do people looking for product and service providers and potential employers. The content is easily searchable, and it is relatively easy to connect to the right people.

Fill out each section carefully. Use the tips I just mentioned for creating your résumé content. Ask people you know to write recommendations for you. Mention your volunteer experience. If you are applying for the type of job that would require a portfolio, you can add it to your LinkedIn profile.

Post updates frequently but not so often that it looks like you spend all day on LinkedIn instead of working. This isn't Facebook where you are posting about personal activities. Talk about what you are working on and mention cool things that your company is doing (as long as you aren't leaking confidential information).

Here are some ideas:

- If your company gets some press, share it as a post.
- If you see an industry article, post the link to it.
- Praise a coworker for great work on a project (consider creating it as a recommendation that will be attached to their LinkedIn profile).
- If your company is running a special promotion or introducing a new product, that is an item worthy of mentioning on LinkedIn.

The purpose of posting is to gain top-of-mind awareness. What you post says a lot about your passion for your industry, dedication to your career, and professionalism. That is an important part of your personal brand.

Professional Photos

The final attention-getting element of your personal brand is your professional photo. When you are building a personal brand, good professional photos are worth the investment. Update them at least every three years.

Your photo session should include several poses and changes of clothing. If your industry is more casual or part of your work day is spent outdoors or in a manufacturing facility, consider having photos taken in the workplace. Be sure to have some formal photos taken in a studio too.

In most cases, you'll probably only need a photo that is cropped to show your head and shoulders (called a head shot). However, it is useful to have shots that include your body from the waist up (like mine on the back of this book). In the next chapter, we'll talk more about reputation-building elements of a personal brand. You'll find other ways to use these photos with the reputation-building elements such as blog posts and articles.

Regardless, your mom would love to have a nice photo of you for the mantle. The last one she has is your senior photo. A photo session with a professional photographer isn't inexpensive. However, it will pay for itself in terms of increased confidence and professionalism.

The résumé, LinkedIn profile, and professional photos are the essential attention-getting elements of your personal brand. They paint a concrete image of you and your qualifications.

In the next chapter, we go deeper with key reputation-building elements that give people an in-depth look at you, your values, your expertise, and your vision for your personal, professional, and community service roles.

10
Craft a Strong Personal Brand: Build Your Reputation

In the last chapter, I walked you through the three most-typical attention-getting elements of your personal brand. But there is more you can do to build your personal brand.

While the three attention-getting elements are considered essential for professionals, the reputation-building elements I'll discuss next are optional. However, if you are the face of your company or you are climbing the corporate ladder, you should consider the reputation-building activities highlighted in this chapter.

I'll discuss blogging and social media specifically but mostly in terms of content development. See, the idea is to build your personal brand as a professional by showcasing your expertise, experience, and value. By writing content, it positions you as a subject matter expert. The nature of your content will often reveal the content of your character, your intellect, your ideas, and your passion for your industry or the customers you serve.

I'll explain blogging, article writing, and social media in general first before I dive deeper into content development.

Platforms for Sharing Content

You may not consider yourself a public speaker or expert but you will find topics in your industry that you believe are crucial to success. They are topics about which you feel passionately.

If you aren't passionate about anything in your industry or your job, you need a career change. Everyone needs to make a living, but it is time for some serious reflection and future planning if you are not passionate about anything you do. You are doing your personal brand more harm than good to stay where you are.

> "Everyone needs to make a living, but it is time for some serious reflection and future planning if you are not passionate about anything you do."

Now that I've got that brief rant out of the way, let's talk about communication platforms for sharing your passion and knowledge about what you do. Those are key pieces of your personal brand. By putting your knowledge out there, you'll give people the opportunity to quote you and to share your articles and blog posts with their peers. You create content that others can discover with a simple search engine query. That helps build your reputation. You never know when that next job offer or client may emerge because someone discovered you on the Internet.

Let's talk about communication platforms where you can share your content.

Blogs

I'm a big fan of blogging. It is easy to set up your own blog. You can go to Blogger.com or Wordpress.com to set up a blog for free or just a small fee. LinkedIn even has a function where you can write a blog post and attach it to your LinkedIn profile. Consider writing guest blog posts for other bloggers who would be interested in your topic.

Blogs are websites programmed to allow interaction between authors and their audiences. Most bloggers allow people to post comments on their blog posts. Search out bloggers who write about your favorite topics. Sign up to receive notifications when they create new blog posts. If you can weigh in on the topic — for or against or just want to share added related content — then comment on the post. Be sure to sign your name and your company name if appropriate. If you have a website or blog of your own, add that link to your signature.

Industry and Professional Association Publications

Another place to share your expertise is in industry and professional association newsletters and magazines. Depending on your company, you may need to get permission from your corporate affairs department. Check with them to ensure you don't violate any company policies.

Reach out to these publications to introduce yourself as a

subject matter expert who would be willing to be interviewed for articles. You can offer to write articles for them as well.

Speaking

Consider speaking at industry association meetings and conference breakout sessions. This is an incredible growth experience. It will develop your speaking skills and help you connect to others in your industry.

Preparation can be time-consuming, but it is a great way to give back to your industry. If you are self-employed, it can put you in front of people who might want to hire you.

Social Media

Social media platforms like Facebook and LinkedIn can provide great ways to share your expertise through your own posts. You can also comment on social media posts of others just like you can on blog posts. Locate LinkedIn and Facebook groups where you can share your own blog posts. Develop a Twitter following by commenting on industry topics and engaging in conversations with other Twitterers who have similar backgrounds and interests. Consider using Pinterest and Instagram to build your brand and create a following if they fit with you goals.

How you use social media depends on the nature of your industry and expertise. Search out well-known figures inside and outside your industry or topic area. Connect with them and study how the integrate these reputation-building elements. Don't steal their ideas — reinvent them.

Videos and Podcasts

Consider recording a series of YouTube videos where you share expertise or interview other subject matter experts. Browse the Internet radio shows on websites such as Blogtalkradio.com and pitch your expertise and topic ideas to radio show hosts.

You can also create podcasts and make them downloadable either on your own website or via websites like iTunes that feature downloadable content.

Writing Content That Positions You As an Expert

> **Written content on the Internet is one of the best ways to build a brand because it allows you to take advantage of the Internet search engines.**

As you saw in the previous section, content doesn't always end up being delivered as the written word. However, written content on the Internet is one of the best ways to build a brand because it allows you to take advantage of the Internet search engines. The content is more sharable when it lives on the Internet, but print articles are helpful as well. Any publicity is valuable when building your reputation.

Once you research the platforms you have available to share your expertise, reach out and offer your assistance. Some will respond. Ask if they have particular topics scheduled.

If publications don't mention article length, ask how long the article should be. You don't want to write a 1,500-word masterpiece when they only have room for 450 words.

Typical word counts vary for each communication platform.

Hard-copy publications are more strict than those online. If you write for an industry publication, local newspaper, or business journal as a guest columnist, they will suggest a desired word count.

You'll find more flexibility with a blog post because it is online content. Blog posts can consist of a photo and five words or even one hundred words. Blog posts are usually no more than one thousand words.

When pursuing newspaper coverage, I pitch it with a press release first. It gives the reporter prepared content that he can cut and paste. That reduces the likelihood of being misquoted. Sometimes the press release will be printed in its entirety. Write it carefully in preparation for that. Everyone wins when you help save the newspaper staff time by providing ready-to-publish content.

You might consider posting commentary or a series of posts on Twitter with content from an article you wrote. I have seen authors tweet the content of their books 140 characters at a time. It's important to learn to create impact in brief blasts to ensure you keep the attention of the people who follow you. You can preprogram your social media posts with applications like Hootsuite.

Grab the reader's attention. Provocative headlines draw in your audience. Shocking statements and questions peak their curiosity.

Promising the reader a number of steps to a better way of life works too. If you Google a topic, you'll find tens and maybe hundreds of articles with headlines like "Six Steps to Financial Freedom" or "Ten Ways to Ask for a Raise." It may seem silly but it works.

Become a student of Internet copy writing. Successful bloggers use tried-and-true copy-writing techniques. Learn from their practices.

When writing on a topic, avoid being too broad. Readers today rarely take the time to read lengthy articles. You will find better readership with short articles on niche topics that appeal to narrow target audiences.

Reader preferences drive changes in how content is written and delivered. Many readers today prefer shorter paragraphs, chapters, and books. Readers feel a great sense of satisfaction when they finish a book, but few find enough time these days to finish reading longer books. This change inspired the design of this book. It is short enough to read on a business trip.

> "You will find better readership with short articles on niche topics that appeal to narrow target audiences."

These are just a few ideas to get you started on the reputation-building elements of your personal brand. People really do want to know what you think. It can be a lot of work; but when you write on a topic about which you are passionate (as I am about the topic of building confidence), the words and ideas come easily.

People are naturally curious and seek out information that will help them. They need your expertise and commentary.

What if you don't have decades of experience. Does that mean that you can't write useful content? Of course not. Browse the Internet and social media websites. People at all levels are writing content.

Blogging has provided a platform for anyone with access to the Internet to write content for the world to read. Bloggers who cannot cook are putting recipes they invented on the Internet. Dogs have Twitter accounts that are more active than most human accounts. It is a communication medium that falls victim to unreliable content and foolishness.

Just because someone puts it on the Internet doesn't make it true — or even good. Well-written, valid content is needed to restore faith in the bulk of the information on the Internet. There is a need for your solid information and commentary on your favorite topic.

Using Social Media to Build an Audience

In today's social media-connected world, it is easy to create shareable content that can travel the Internet and put you on the radar of people around the globe. If you give readers a way to connect with you and your content that is appealing enough, you gain them as audience members.

Notice that I said *appealing*; not necessarily intellectual. *Appealing* can mean interesting, funny, or problem-solving. It just needs to appeal to their needs or interests.

If you want to appeal to a particular target audience, get to know them very well — interests, demographics, values, stores they shop, websites they frequent, or magazines they read. Then write content that they want to read, and write it in a way they would find appealing.

Again, your content might not be the written word at all. It might be a video or podcast. You should deliver it via whatever medium your target audience prefers to use to consume it. And don't forget to post it on social media so people can share it with their connections.

If building a reputation for you or your company is your goal, gather all the knowledge you can to stay fresh and relevant. If you run a business or you are climbing the corporate ladder, reputation-building is worth your time.

At each place in your career, you have multiple topics you can study and write about. Choose a topic and spend thirty minutes a day reading on the topic. Within a year, you will know more about that topic than 90 percent of the people in the world.

This isn't intended to be a replacement for specialized education and certification required by many fields such as neurosurgery or mechanical engineering. However, even those professionals need to stay current and relevant on their expertise. Consuming thirty minutes of information on their topic of choice daily will move them to the front of their field.

Writing transforms the way you feel about yourself. It becomes much easier to feel confident in your abilities when the evidence of your knowledge appears in black and white.

When you turn the information you learn into commentary or content that helps others, you become known for your expertise. And that is how reputations and personal brands are built.

Spelling, Grammar, and Punctuation Alert

If you struggle with writing and all the rules of basic English, consider hiring someone to edit your written content before you post it. You can dictate your information and send it to a writer to type, edit, and even post. You may be a genius but people will tear your ideas apart more readily if your posts are loaded with typos.

As an alternative, have someone come behind you and edit your social media posts. Twitter doesn't allow editing but all the other social media platforms do. Hiring someone with writing and editing skills to log in on your accounts and clean up your errors can save your reputation.

A Word on Social Media Exposure

Always treat everything you post as public. You may have your Facebook privacy settings locked down; but your not-so-nice "friends" can cut and paste your text and download your photos to upload again somewhere else.

Don't show too much skin on photos, be positive in your interactions, and reflect before responding to negativity.

The World Needs Your Content

As I close out this chapter, you might be wondering, "Don't other people already write on this subject? Is there room for another expert on this topic?" Maybe other people — famous people — write on the same or a very similar topic, but there is only one you. Only you can add your perspective or your personal spin on the topic. Only you can deliver it in your special way.

Every well-known expert started out as a virtual unknown. There has never been a better time to build an audience and a personal brand by sharing your expertise, ideas, and insights.

11
Volunteer to Build Confidence in Your Abilities

I spent fifteen years of my career working for large companies. Most of those were the years when I was also raising a family and working on my college education. There wasn't a lot of time left over to serve my community.

Volunteering was something I wanted to do; but outside participating in some small fund-raisers at work, the opportunity never really presented itself.

In 2001, I found myself with a newly blended family that needed me home worse than we needed my paycheck. We had worked hard to pay off our cars, student loan, and credit cards. We were just about $300 month short of being able to afford for me to stay home. I took the risk anyway, and I stepped away from my regular paycheck. I don't know how we managed, but we always made the bills.

Our debt-free life provided me with something a lot of

people my age didn't have — options. I chose to be available for my family on a full-time basis. We had quality of life that we never had while I worked full time. I could concentrate on completing a Masters in Business Administration program and help my daughter with the demands of school. I even had some extra time to serve in my community. Finally, I could volunteer for some local organizations.

I volunteered alongside my husband leading church Bible studies and went on a mission trip to India. Those were a nice way to tip my toe in the water. I felt like I could do more though.

I was new to volunteering and I didn't know what I really wanted to do. I looked for ways to volunteer at my daughter's school. I volunteered as with the band boosters and ended up serving as a copresident with a friend. That gave me a chance to spend more time with my daughter, encourage her with my involvement, and get to know the kids she hung around with. In junior high school, those are all very important.

I continued to scope out volunteer opportunities. I had learned about SCORE when I started my first business in Texas in 1992. It is a volunteer organization that provides small business mentoring services for free. I had grown up in a small business family as did both of my parents. Helping small businesses succeed was a cause I was passionate about.

With some small business start-up and marketing education, expertise, and experience as well as the ability to coach people on writing business plans, I had something to offer. Most of the SCORE members were older than my parents, but they gladly welcomed me.

I enjoyed networking and knew I wanted to run my own business again. I was still exploring different business ideas and finishing my MBA. It would be two years before I felt like I had the time and stability at home to finally start a business.

Like a lot of people who leave the workforce to stay home, I felt like I was adrift at first. It's pretty common for someone who had always worked to base her worth on her paycheck or her title. My community was the group of people with whom I worked. I wasn't really tight with anyone outside work when I left my full-time job.

> "My volunteer work allowed me to try my hand at some things I'd never done. I didn't have a lot of management experience at that point. Jumping in to volunteer like I did gave me the chance to build a leadership résumé."

My husband was supportive and generous, but things were very challenging with my daughter. She was struggling with anxiety and depression and school problems. It was a strange time where it felt like there was no balance. I left my job to find some balance, yet my life felt less balanced than ever.

My volunteer work was enjoyable and challenging. It provided a way to use my skills and find some satisfaction in serving others outside my family. It allowed me to try my hand at some things I'd never done. I didn't have a lot of management experience at that point. Jumping in to volunteer like I did gave me the chance to build a leadership résumé.

Over the next fourteen years, I held leadership roles in over twenty organizations. I developed a network of hundreds of people where anything I needed was a referral or two away if it wasn't already at my fingertips. I recruited teams, created new fund-raising events, and dealt with tougher ethical challenges than I ever faced working in a company. I built a network of peers who provided accountability and feedback when I was struggling with the inherent gray areas of volunteer leadership.

I nearly always fell into leadership roles quickly when I found an organization I could help. Usually it was because no one else wanted to lead.

I liked the challenge of leadership, and nonprofits were always glad to have the help. I brought some useful skills to the table — mostly my project management skills and my vast network. I used to joke, "What are they going to do if I make a mistake — fire me?" It seemed like a reasonably low risk, and I found a lot of personal satisfaction from each experience. With each assignment, my confidence in my capabilities grew.

As my business I started in 2003 grew, I learned to focus my volunteer activities to get the most volunteer value for the time I had to invest. My responsibilities grew as my leadership capabilities developed.

I ran for public office in 2012 and pulled together my community service résumé. I had not realized until then that I had built a substantial leadership portfolio working for free and leading teams of people who worked for free. Together, we served mighty missions.

Each experience prepared me for the next. I learned to make decisions without all the information. I learned to identify what I didn't know and how to get help to address that weakness. I loved working alongside people who weren't afraid to get their hands dirty. Occasionally I would make mistakes and missteps. I learned how to resolve them efficiently. I would have to identify and address ethical issues. All provided great learning experiences.

There would be the occasional recruiting mistake on the team that would result in conflict. And occasionally a volunteer accepted an assignment and then experienced a life change that prevented them from honoring their commitment. I learned how to help volunteers out of the assignment they accepted when necessary. They were always grateful and their reputations remained intact. We had a lot of successes together but the mistakes, challenges, people issues, and frustrations taught me the most.

Determining Where and How to Volunteer

Volunteering will give you the greatest opportunity to develop your confidence. Here are some important criteria to consider when choosing where to volunteer.

Causes

Ask yourself what causes you are passionate about. Research local organizations that serve those causes. You can find a partial list on your local chamber of commerce and United Way websites. There are many local charities that are not listed there, but those will get you started.

Skills

Ask yourself what skills you'd like to use as a volunteer. You can bring your current skills to the table. If you want to develop a skill to add to your professional résumé, seek out opportunities to try something new.

Tasks You Won't Do

Ask yourself what you don't want to do. If you don't want to make phone calls or ask for money, make that clear with organizations you talk with. There are plenty of places that can use your time in the way you want to volunteer.

Time

Ask yourself what kind of time you can commit. This can shift throughout the year. If you want to get the most out of your volunteer experience, choose one organization and volunteer in larger roles versus working only the day of an event for several organizations.

Larger roles such as board membership or working on an event-planning committee will lead to a stronger network of contacts and deeper relationships.

Be realistic about your available time and the needs of a particular activity. For instance, if you work in retail and Christmas is when you work the most hours, don't volunteer to organize a Christmas activity that requires tons of time during the fourth quarter of the year.

Research and Identify Compatibility

Meet with organizations after you've researched their

website to learn about their mission and activities. Find out where they need help and inquire about ways they can use your skills. Ask all the questions you can think of.

With each assignment and organization, you learn a bit more about assessing whether you and the organization are compatible. They may be desperate for someone with your skill set, but you don't want to get into an assignment where you are miserable or won't do your best work. It will make you look bad, and it will let them down.

Your Mission

Write a mission statement for each volunteer assignment. It is so easy to take on too much when you volunteer. You can get in over your head. When you determine up front what you want to do, it sets boundaries.

When faced with taking on an additional task, you can weigh it against your mission statement. If it fits and you have time, then take it. If it doesn't — even if you have plenty of available time — say no.

Commitment

Give the organizations with whom you work a time commitment. I always committed a year at a time. Sure, I worked longer if I served them well and I still had more to offer. I had several assignments where I served four years or more.

The one-year time commitment gave me a way out if something wasn't the right fit or I just didn't feel like my values aligned with the organization. Over time, I learned to prescreen for potential issues so I could avoid a failed volunteer relationship from the start. In the beginning, you don't know what you don't know.

The Confidence to Accept the Calling

I've known a lot of people over the years who didn't consider themselves a leader. They started out helping on a committee. Then they worked into small leadership roles that led to larger leadership roles.

They might have had the capability all the time but not the confidence in themselves. But as they built confidence in one role, they felt confident enough to accept a new role. Over time, they forgot they ever lacked confidence. They instead asked themselves how they can help or learn something new. What initially felt like a huge risk they wanted to *run from* became a challenge they *run to*.

Volunteer work creates unlikely heroes. Will you be the next one?

12
Make Meaningful Conversation

Remember that first day of junior high when you walked on campus for the first time? You stood before a new school that was bigger than the last. It was unfamiliar territory.

You scanned the school grounds in search of someone you recognized. Groups of students were talking and laughing. You had a million questions of self-doubt racing through your mind.

Did you have the right school supplies? You couldn't get the exact package of colored pencils they asked for. Was it okay to have the pocket folder with the brads even though it asked for the plain pocket folder? Why didn't your mom take you shopping for school supplies sooner?

Were you wearing the right clothes? You spent all week planning what you were going to wear on the first day of school. Why didn't you see more people wearing the same kind of jeans?

How would you know where to get your schedule? Would you be able to find your classrooms?

And what was up with this pimple on your nose, the biggest one in months? Ugh.

Where are your friends from your old school? These people look so much cooler than you. What if no one wants to sit with you at lunch?

Does that sound like the monologue in your head when you walk into a new place or gathering for the first time? What is it about new experiences that take us back to the first day of junior high?

Similar questions taunt us when we walk into a networking group or social event. Where are those people you already know? Are you dressed the right way for the event? Where is the event in this big hotel? You forgot your business cards — should you even bother to go?

You may think you are the only adult who still feels this way. The truth is that we never really grow out of the feeling of uncertainty we experienced on the first day of junior high. Understanding how to manage that fear and anxiety will ensure that you capture every chance at a successful life.

The decisions you make when you enter a room often set the stage for your future. They are the fragments of achievement that become the mosaic of confident living. John Wayne once said, "Courage is being scared to death and saddling up anyway."

Let me speak some truth into that angst-filled moment when you go walk into a new place.

First, you are the only one who thinks you are a goober. Everyone in the room walks in with the same negative self-talk in their head. No one is worried about what anyone else looks like. They are worried they are the biggest goober in the room.

People in that situation look for a comfort zone. For some, a comfort zone is taking a seat at a table in the room and scanning their smart phone e-mail or social media apps. Sometimes it is the food line. Some find their comfort zone by grabbing an alcoholic drink and standing against the wall. A popular comfort zone is standing with someone they already know. Their comfort zone definitely does not involve initiating the conversation with someone new, even though that is probably the reason they attend such an event.

When you come prepared with a plan for making meaningful conversation, you not only look confident, you are saving others from the anxiety they also feel.

> "When you come prepared with a plan for making meaningful conversation, you not only look confident, you are saving others from the anxiety they also feel."

Second, those groups of people standing around already know each other. That is why they look like they are having a great time. They found their comfort zone. They stand glued to each other like they are clinging for life. They don't meet anyone new. They don't even talk about anything but small talk.

They are missing the most important chance of the day: the

opportunity to expand their network. Those formed groups are difficult for new people to break into, so it almost guarantees those in the tightly snuggled group won't meet anyone new. The same thing happens at civic club meetings where the same people sit at the same table each week.

During the 2008 presidential primary election season, I heard political analyst Bob Schiefer say that running for president was a lot like running for student council in high school. Likability was a major contributor in a voter's choice of candidate.

Likability matters in all areas of our lives, and it is attainable for even the biggest introvert. Here is the secret to being likeable: knowing how to make meaningful conversation. When you can initiate and lead a conversation, you have the power to be not only likeable but memorable.

When you lead a meaningful conversation, what I'm suggesting is that you ask a series of open-ended questions. Those are questions that can't be answered with a simple *yes* or *no*. Open-ended questions generally provide responses that be woven together into a conversation. Each response should trigger the next open-ended question to gather more information.

Here are some examples of open-ended questions:

- What did you do this weekend?
- Where is your daughter working this summer?
- How did you end up in your current job?

Taking responsibility for leading the conversation puts the other person at ease. They don't have to worry about what they are going to say next. They are more likely to remember they met you because their level of anxiety is significantly reduced.

It also makes them feel honored that you would take the time to ask questions about them. It proves you care. I mentioned this quote in an earlier chapter: "People don't care how much you know until they know how much you care." When you show you care, your likability rating goes way up.

Meaningful conversation has yet another purpose. You get the information you need to know how to create the next steps in the relationship. Who is in their network? Do they serve the same type of client you do? Are they a potential client for you or someone else in your network?

It gives you reasons to follow up later. When you know more about someone, it gives business owners and salespeople creative ideas to follow up that go way beyond asking, "Are you ready to do business with me yet?

The same is true if you are networking for career change or just expanding your network of connections. When you have reasons to follow up, you can reach out to the person more often. You show you authentically care about their interests. It makes a lasting impression that may lead to introductions to other people you need to meet.

Here is an important truth for people who network for business: people don't do business with us for all kinds of reasons. They may not need our product or service right now. They may realize they need us. They may not be able to afford us.

Being able to find reasons to build a deeper relationship over time creates top-of-mind awareness and trust. When they finally have the need or, better yet, meet someone who has the need for you or your product or service, they will remember you.

I designed the template for leading meaningful conversation that I teach in all my programs. It gets rave reviews from introverts as well as extroverts. It gives you a list of questions that you can memorize and ask every time you meet someone new. You will find it useful with people you already know too. It's just crazy how we schlep into the same office every day with the same people and we don't know very much about them. Start the conversation.

Here is the template of questions I use when meeting business professionals. You'll find it adapts easily to all types of people:

> "Hi! I'm [your name]." [She will respond with her name usually. If she doesn't, it is okay to ask her name.]
>
> "What do you do? What company are you with?"
>
> "What is your role at [her organization]?"
>
> "How long have you been with your company [or owned it]?"
>
> "Tell me more about what your company does." [Listen to understand. Ask questions about the organization until you understand what the organization does.]
>
> "Who is your ideal client?"
>
> "Are you from this area?" [People usually offer information about where they are from if they aren't from the area.]

[If not from the area] **"What brings you to this area?"**

[If the last question revealed she moved to the area because of a spouse's job] **"What does your spouse do?"**

"Do you have family in the area?" [This may reveal children, spouse, siblings, or parents that you can inquire about.]

"Are you involved in any charities?" [Question her further if she says yes. You may also discover she would like to volunteer somewhere but doesn't know where she fits in. Keeping up with local nonprofits allows you to offer ideas.]

"What do you do in your free time?"

Begin your close: **"It was great to meet you. Do you have a business card so I can refer you if I meet anyone who needs to know you?"** [Usually people will ask you for your business card. You may offer your card when they don't ask. You can also follow up later with your business card tucked inside a handwritten note.]

Normally at this point, the conversation turns around to you. The individual feels comfortable enough to start asking some questions. If she doesn't, that's fine. She may be in a hurry or is still nervous about meeting someone new or just not very skilled at making conversation. It is hardly ever a sign that someone doesn't care about you. You are armed with lots of information that will make it easier to initiate future conversations to deepen the relationship.

I give many more ideas for making conversation in my book

Currency: Striking Networking Gold in a Relationship Economy. You can learn more about it in the back of this book.

The beauty of using a template is that you know what you are going to say next. You can lead that conversation with a plan for what you'll ask. This frees your attention to focus on what the other person is saying. You are much more likely to remember names and other key details of the conversation for later follow up.

You are going to be great at making conversation. You will make a likeable, confident, and memorable impression.

13
Free Your Voice

I worked for a corporate employee magazine for almost five years. Our managing editor usually delivered the overview of our department at the monthly orientation for new field managers. She was going to be gone for the next one, so she asked if I would do it. It was a ten-minute talk, and I just needed to share what we did. No problemo. I had this.

I remember standing in front of my mirror in the bathroom at home, practicing the presentation I had prepared. I imagined them leaning forward eagerly, hanging on to every single word. I was brilliant and engaging. I just knew this was the first of many, many presentations because surely people would want me to speak to other groups too. I had long dreamed of being a public speaker. Wow! This talk was the beginning of great things.

The moment of truth arrived — my ten minutes of pure genius that I was about to deliver. I walked in a few minutes early and sat in the back of the room. I hoped to manage my butterflies. Actually, I scanned the room for a trash can to puke in if I couldn't make a quick enough escape to the restroom.

The meeting facilitator called me up to the front of the room and introduced me. I looked out at a group of a dozen people clearly suffering from a post-lunch food coma. I began to feel my neck rash out and my throat tighten. As I struggled to speak, my voice felt very small. People began to lean forward just so they could better hear what I was saying.

I could not remember anything I was supposed to say, so I proceeded to stammer and fumble with my notes. I dropped the stack of magazines that I brought to distribute. I think one guy might have been preparing to catch me if I passed out. I'm not sure who was more horrified — me or the audience. It felt like sixty minutes of pure terror.

Oh my. What a disaster! It didn't go at all like it did in front of my bathroom mirror.

Have you ever tripped and fallen, and it seemed like it was happening in very slow motion? You know how the fall keeps playing over and over in your head? Every time it plays, the memory of it seems a little more awkward and foolish. If you got lucky, no one was there to watch you fall — or at least anyone you know.

My failed presentation was playing over and over in my head. Each time, I winced a little harder.

I wasn't lucky enough to embarrass myself without an audience. I might not see these people again, but the meeting facilitator worked in my area.

Speakers always stress out over things that we wish we'd done differently on the platform. We blow mistakes way out of proportion that no one else notices. Not only did I not meet my expectations, my presentation was growing to a disaster of epic proportion in my head.

I was crushed. I didn't attempt to speak in front of a group of any size for at least two years. I barely had the courage to speak up in department meetings. [Sigh.]

I eventually talked my supervisor into paying for me to take the *Dale Carnegie Course*. It is a human relations course, but there is a lot of public speaking practice over the twelve-week program. It was a win-win. I wanted to develop my public speaking skills. My supervisor wanted me to develop my human relations skills.

It made a big difference. I wouldn't say I was a good public speaker afterward, but I enjoyed feeling more confident about speaking up.

A few years later, I was invited to visit a Toastmasters club. I politely declined. It wasn't the right time for me, and I was a good enough speaker to get by.

Eventually, I decided that getting by wasn't good enough. I wanted to conquer my fear of public speaking and use my voice, my expertise, and my experience to help others improve their lives.

I joined a Toastmasters club and got involved. I gave speeches and served in leadership roles. The speeches honed all the elements of my public speaking skills. Serving as a Toastmasters leader at the club and district level gave me many opportunities to hone my human relations skills. I got all that for a fraction of the cost of the *Dale Carnegie Course* — something that I liked since I was self-employed by that time.

It is really easy to choose a path that is flat and straight. There's no anxiety, and you know exactly what to expect. The problem is that it never challenges you to improve.

It is normal to experience fear and anxiety. It is normal to make mistakes. Those things are the markers along the journey between the starting line and a confident you. Conquering fear and anxiety and learning from risks and mistakes are what teach you the most.

Are you someone who is satisfied to say, "I'm not a good public speaker," and settle for a life where your voice and your ideas are kept tucked away in a tiny box? Prolonging the journey to become a better public speaker serves no one. It can keep you from experiencing all you could accomplish as a confident speaker.

Free your voice by developing your public speaking skills. The world needs to hear your voice sharing your expertise, experiences, and ideas. There's no time like now to get started.

14
Define Your Personal Truth

I began speaking and writing on the interconnected topics of marketing, communication, networking, and business relationships in 2002. I searched for and developed information and techniques that would help my audiences. Over the years, I've developed programs for corporate professionals, business owners, salespeople, job searchers, and nonprofit executives.

I frequently encountered people with a mental speed bump that eventually became a roadblock to success. It kept them from moving forward and succeeding. I couldn't pinpoint why some were able to overcome challenges while others could not. The people who struggled seemed to suffer from an issue rooted in low-self esteem, but I always sensed something more haunted them.

It wasn't until 2010 that a client project reminded me of 1902 study I had read about years earlier. It resulted in a theory called *The Looking Glass Self* created by researcher Charles Horton Cooley.

The study revealed that people base their perceptions of themselves on what they think other people think of them. The phenomenon begins at an early age and continues throughout a person's life unless all social interactions cease.

There were three major components of the theory:

- We imagine how we appear to others.
- We imagine the judgment of that appearance.
- We develop our self through the judgments of others.

Let's rephrase that:

We base what we think about ourselves
> **on what we think**
>> **other people think** about us.

Not what they told us they think about us. Not what we know to be true about ourselves. What we THINK other people think about us.

That sounds a little silly, doesn't it?

Here's how this plays out in real life.

Jane is interviewing for a great job. The description matches her credentials. She even brings some experience that most candidates will not. She knows she is the most qualified candidate they will interview. She brought three copies of her résumé printed on fine parchment paper. She arrives ten minutes early for the interview wearing her best suit. It is smartly tailored and professional. She checks in with the receptionist and takes her place confidently in the waiting room.

A gentleman walks out of his office to talk with the receptionist. She appears to mention that Jane is his next appointment. With a frown on his face, he looks over at Jane. She gives him a polite wave. He then leaves the room for a few minutes.

Suddenly, things change for Jane. The voices of self-doubt flood her thoughts.

> "The hiring manager has probably already made his decision, and he is just doing this as a courtesy interview."
>
> "I'm dressed a lot differently than the other people here. Maybe I wore the wrong outfit."
>
> "I'm probably not as qualified as I thought."
>
> "I bet I'm not going to get this job."
>
> "Maybe he'd prefer to hire a man for the job."
>
> "I don't know if I'm the right fit for this company."

How well do you think her interview is going to go? She has just changed what she believes about herself and her capabilities based on what she thinks someone else thinks about her.

He's the sad realization: that frown on his face probably has nothing to do with her. Maybe he just learned a family member died. Maybe he had an argument with his son on the phone. Maybe he is just GASSY.

Oh my goodness! Jane could now think that she is not worthy of such a great career move and ruin her chances at delivering the best interview of her life because the hiring manager's lunch didn't agree with him.

The Looking Glass Self theory opened my eyes to the cause of the roadblock to success I saw people experience. They could never achieve their full potential until they believed the very best about themselves. They could not build a strong personal brand, achieve their goals, or even make a confident first impression because they didn't believe in their own capabilities.

You must make the first sale to yourself. Until you do, no one else will buy.

This was a turning point for me in how I helped my clients. Now I understood how to help my clients change what they believed about themselves.

> "No matter how difficult they were, I found that the more I reviewed these phrases — written as if I had already accomplished them — the more possible they seemed. The more I believed it was possible, the truer each statement became."

Eliminating the Negative Self-Talk

Once a year, I sit down and write my goals. They are specific, measurable, action-oriented, realistic, and time-bound — just like management consultant Peter Drucker spoke of in his Management by Objective concept.

A few years ago, I noticed I carried over some of the same goals each year. I had already accomplished them, but I kept them on the list. When we get busy, it is easy to get distracted by that which is urgent. It shakes up our routine of doing those things that made us successful.

Carrying over these goals was my way of maintaining habits that helped me achieve success.

I noticed that I wrote these phrases differently since they were "accomplished goals." They were still quantifiable but written as present-time practices. They typically represented a value I held dear or a habit that I wanted to maintain like:

> I honor and nurture God's gift of life by exercising at least fifteen minutes and eating at least two healthy meals each day.
>
> I base decisions on principle rather than emotion.

I decided to experiment with writing some goals that were phrased as if I was already doing them. I wrote some to address areas of needed improvement. These targeted tardiness, client follow-up, and a need be more positive in periods of adversity. Here was the result:

> I arrive at my destination fifteen minutes early.
>
> I actively prospect and aggressively follow up with my business prospects.
>
> I express my gratitude for my challenges and lessons as well as my blessings and opportunities.

When I reviewed these phrases, I read them as if that goal, habit, or value was something I already accomplished and practiced as part of my daily routine.

No matter how difficult they were, I found that the more I reviewed these phrases — written as if I had already accomplished them — the more possible they seemed. The more I believed it was possible, the truer each statement became. Interestingly, other people also believed these statements about me were true.

Eventually, I owned new beliefs about myself and what I could accomplish. I realized that what I had done was to create a new set of personal truths. This was incredibly powerful for me.

Now my personal truths are organized separately from my goals, but I regularly review them together.

I also developed a three-step process for helping clients replace their negative self-talk with new personal truths.

Step 1: Stop Making Assumptions

If you are curious about what someone thinks, ask them. When they compliment you, take it to heart and say "thank you." It takes a great deal of courage to give feedback of any kind. You must ask for it and create a safe place for people to give it.

And when you get it, thank them. Ask for clarification and listen carefully for meaning. Again, don't make any assumptions. Keep asking questions until you fully understand. It will help you process what you do well and also what you need to improve.

I find it comforting to acknowledge the fact that people don't really think about us that much. They are often more worried about what other people are thinking about them. The more I mention that, the sillier it sounds. But it is true.

Step 2: Brainstorm the Focus for Your Personal Truths

Your personal truths should address a combination of who

you are, what you do, what you value and need, and what you need to improve. The most important phrases are those that address characteristics and qualities.

You also need personal truths for what you already do well so you can ensure continued success in that area.

Here are four questions to ask when brainstorming your personal truths.

- What are two things you do really well? If you don't know, ask a friend, coworker, or former supervisor. You can also review a recent work evaluation for ideas.
- What are two things that you consider necessities? These are things that you need to maintain or obtain. If your life contained these things, it would be a great life.
- What are two values you hold dear?
- What are two behaviors or practices you need to improve?

Step 3: Write Your Personal Truths as If They Already Happen

Create your personal truths in positive, forward-looking, action-oriented language — as if they are already something you do well.

Writing personal truths is a great way to change practices and attitudes that hold you back from your ultimate vision for your life. We are more successful at eliminating bad habits when we replace them with new, improved habits. And because this process is a lot like writing a vision statement for your business, you'll write it as if the new practice or habit is already happening. It's okay to write the phrase as if you are working on that new behavior instead if you prefer. It would look like this:

> *I strive* to base decisions on principle rather than emotion.

Like a goal, a personal truth must be quantifiable so it clearly shows what successful execution of that personal truth looks like.

Here are some examples of answers to each of the questions in Step 2.

Example of a Personal Truth for Something You Do Well

What I Do Well: Showing my gratitude to people

Personal Truth: I brag on people in person and send handwritten notes to tell people I appreciate them.

Example of a Personal Truth for a Value You Hold Dear

A Value I Hold Dear: Doing the right thing

Personal Truth: I uphold a solid moral and ethical reputation.

Example of a Personal Truth for Attaining a Necessity

Something I Need: My health

Personal Truth: I honor and nurture God's gift of life by exercising and eating healthy food.

Example of a Personal Truth for a Behavior or Practice You Need to Improve

A Behavior or Practice to Improve: I spend too much time on Facebook and don't return my e-mails as quickly as I should.

Personal Truth: I return daily e-mails and phone calls before I spend time on social media.

Taking the Next Steps for Success

We tend to get what we expect, and it's no surprise we probably won't get what we don't ask for. We have to create a vision for our life if we want to move forward. Writing personal truths will help you do that.

You might be skeptical. That's understandable because, after all, these are just words. When you read them every day with this fresh, positive phrasing as if they already happen, something powerful happens in our brain. The more we read them, the more they seem possible. Eventually, they start to form permanent change and the new personal truths begin to define us.

Follow these next steps:

- Write your personal truths.
- Post them in a place you will see them every day such as your closet door or at your desk.
- Read them every day.
- Share them with someone else so they can hold you accountable.

You are really going to grow from this process. Prepare to be amazed at the new you that emerges.

15
Lead Well-Organized Face-to-Face Meetings

There is great power in knowing how to plan and lead a meeting. There is even greater power in taking the initiative to call the meeting.

It is worth offering to plan a meeting with your team, even when you are the newest team member in the organization. It gives you a chance to offer needed help and develop your organizational skills. Your top team member may not turn loose of the meeting-planning duties, but you will surely be invited to assist.

There is little difference between planning a one-on-one meeting with a client and a group meeting with your work team. You are working with the same goals in mind:

- To connect
- To accomplish things together
- To create an interactive springboard for ideas and contributions
- To be a good steward of everyone's time.

When you accomplish all four goals, people never leave the meeting thinking, "I'll never get that hour of my life back. What a waste of my time! That was another meeting that could have been accomplished with an e-mail."

Unfortunately, many workplaces use a communication meeting that receives comments like those. Let's call it the "team update meeting."

In this type of meeting, each attendee gives an activity update; someone tells employees about a benefit or policy change; and the leader closes with some atta-boys. Those gatherings are intended to brief the team and meet compliance criteria. It is true that the content of the meeting could probably be delivered by e-mail.

Team update meetings exist because people don't always read an e-mail or paper memo. The gatherings allow people to ask questions and gain more understanding. They are a necessary evil in the workplace, but they accomplish little outside information dissemination.

In contrast, project committees and client meetings allow people to work together to accomplish something bigger than they could alone.

These meetings are most productive when conducted face to face. It is not always possible to get everyone in the same physical location. Today's video, teleconferencing, and online meeting technology allow team members to connect and contribute despite their distance.

The same meeting management principles apply to these virtual meetings.

A Note about Protocol

While there is merit to following *Robert's Rules of Order,* it is far too structured for typical nonprofit and business meetings. I have seen it keep people from participating because they didn't understand when they could contribute.

The basic rules and organization of *Robert's Rules of Order* are helpful as you prepare to facilitate meetings. However, I've found it is easier to develop the skills used to create an environment that invites contribution and arrives at decisions without hard protocol. Meeting management skills help leaders build confidence.

There are some organizations such as political clubs and some boards that have strict meeting structure requirements. Those often involve rules like when meetings are scheduled, attendees are notified, and minutes are approved and filed. I'm not covering those specifics here. This chapter is intended for all the other meetings of the world that accomplish mighty feats unfettered by bureaucracy.

Planning and Running Productive Meetings

A solid meeting plan provides the structure needed for conducting productive meetings. Here are some tips.

- When calling the meeting, give the reason for meeting and the desired outcome.
- Ask for agenda items from the invited individuals ahead of time. This will allow you gauge the length of the meeting (or whether a meeting is even necessary).
- Send out the agenda via e-mail. If you are dealing with

group members who do not use e-mail or other communication technology, you'll need to mail it or personally deliver it.

- Encourage refreshments. Consider delegating that responsibility on a rotating basis.
- Write the agenda on a piece of large notepaper or white board in the meeting room before the meeting starts.
- Start the meeting by thanking everyone for their time. Cover the reason for the meeting and the tasks you hope to accomplish.
- At the beginning of the meeting, mention what time the meeting is scheduled to finish. Ask everyone if they can stay until the end. This alerts you to agenda items that might need to be shuffled.
- Keep the agenda on track to ensure productive use of everyone's time. Gentle reminders help keep people on topic and on schedule.
- Ensure that the group is doing more than reporting progress. People enjoy solving problems and designing solutions together. Create opportunities for the group members to engage in discussion. This also teaches them how to facilitate discussion.
- Schedule the next meeting during the current meeting when possible. Discuss the agenda for the next meeting before dismissing the group.
- If this group meets on a regular basis, confirm with the members that the next meeting is needed.
- At the end of the meeting, thank everyone again for their contributions. Explain what follow up is expected.
- Close the meeting on time.

Understanding the Unspoken Rules of Meeting Leadership

I've assembled a few tips to maintain your position as leader of the meeting.

- The meeting leader should stand when opening the meeting and delivering opening remarks. It is also ideal for the leader to stand during closing remarks to give the meeting a clean finish.
- Project committee and team meetings are not keynote addresses to an audience. The meeting leader facilitates discussion and spends as little time talking as possible.
- During the course of the meeting, encourage people to stand when speaking.
- Standing during meeting facilitation allows you to move around. This can be helpful in managing team member participation. Making eye contact or attaining close physical proximity encourages a quiet team member to interact and speak his ideas. This is much better than simply calling on him to speak.
- In contrast, moving to break eye contact or give a physical sign can quiet a team member who over-participates. Just walking up behind him with a simple touch on his shoulder while you are talking to the group can lower his activity level.
- If you lead the organization or team but allow different members to run the meeting, you should continue to start and end the meeting. This ensures that you are positioned as the leader in everyone's mind. It is a subtle but powerful signal.
- If you are invited to be a guest presenter at someone

else's meeting, make sure you stand when you give your presentation. This shows respect to the group members and positions you as a confident leader and subject matter expert in the audience members' minds. Even when everyone else is sitting, never sit while giving your presentation.

Using Guest Meeting Organizers

If you have a meeting that happens on a regular basis, rotate the responsibility to plan and run it among different group members. This is a great way to share responsibility. It also provides hands-on meeting management training. Here are some tips to help guest organizers and leaders succeed.

- Consider allowing the guest meeting organizer to set the agenda and plan the details of the meeting. This is a great way to teach people how to plan and run productive meetings.
- Be sure to check in periodically with guest meeting organizers to ensure plans are going well. They might be hesitant to ask for help so watch for warning signs.
- Debrief with guest meeting organizers after the meeting. Ask them what they thought went well and if they had any challenges. If they need some tips for improvement for next time, remember to be gentle and encouraging as this is a training opportunity. Thank them for their effort.

Whether you are planning one-on-one meetings (such as those with clients, mentors, or supervisors) or a group meetings (like those with your work team, a fund-raising committee, or a Bible study), you can ensure that participants remain excited, engaged, and active with proper planning and organization.

16
Step Up and Grab That Microphone

We've all heard someone say this when they've been handed a microphone: "Oh I don't need that. I'll just use my teacher voice."

I'm going to hurt some feelings with this chapter, but if this is for everyone's own good — those who speak and those who listen.

The "teacher voice" option isn't really an option — it's a cover-up for low-self esteem. It's mostly used by women with low-esteem. And not just that, it is a sad indicator of how society feels that somehow someone with a microphone is worthy of having something to say. When you turn down the chance to use it, you are conveying that what you have to say isn't that important.

No one wants to hear anyone's "teacher voice." It is screechy and strained. It lacks real emotion and inflection. When teachers use it, someone is in trouble and too many people are misbehaving for a teacher to be heard. Nothing attached to a "teacher voice" is anything that makes us feel good. It's memorable all right, but it isn't a good memory.

Too much of the impact of your message comes from the emotion and inflection of your voice. The worst thing we can do is to turn away a microphone that can amplify our emotion and inflection. Turning it away reduces our power.

Having worked in the professional speaking industry since 2003, I learned where the greatest power resides in a speaker's message. There are many nuances that go unnoticed by people outside the industry.

I call your attention now to some power points to consider when you are handed the microphone. These power points have nothing to do with Microsoft PowerPoint® software.

These power points are truths you can use to add power to your message.

Power Point 1: Gestures, Stage Positioning, and Stance

The way the speaker uses his or her body — gestures, stage positioning, and stance — are critical in delivering a powerful message.

The speaker's use of gestures embellishes the visual, the word picture, and the punctuation. Gestures should flow naturally. Be careful to hold the microphone close to your mouth. Resist the urge to gesture with it.

Stage positioning changes moods, signals transitions in the story, and connects the speaker to the audience.

Stance communicates emotion as much as gestures do. When you want to look confident, stand tall with legs shoulder-width apart. I call it my superhero stance.

Power Point 2: The Power of the Platform

Simply standing in front of an audience positions you as a leader in the minds of audience members. When you've been invited to speak to a group, attendees have great expectations that the meeting organizers have planned an unforgettable meeting experience. They wouldn't invite anyone less than wonderful for such an important task, would they?

Power Point 3: People Hold Speakers in High Regard

Because most people fear public speaking more than anything else, they view those who are courageous enough to speak as superheroes.

This sets the stage for you to make a difference in someone's life when you invest the time and risk involved in developing speaking skills.

Those skills aren't built by imagining how a speech might go or by practicing in front of a mirror. We build speaking chops by practicing in front of live audiences. Toastmasters is a club that helps members develop communication and leadership skills. It is inexpensive, and there are clubs all over the world. Visit www.toastmasters.org to find a club near you.

Power Point 4: Speakers Often Overlook How Powerful Their Message Is

Speakers are overly self-critical of every word they say. How we remember our speeches went is nearly always much different than how it actually happened.

I record my speeches with a small digital recorder and lapel microphone so I can listen to them later. It is a good development tool, but listening to the recording proves the foibles I made didn't ruin the speech at all. The recorder also captures those unplanned moments of magic in my message that might have been forgotten afterward.

Over time, often years, speakers begin to recognize the impact of their ideas and spoken words. As time goes by, they realize the unplanned words and verbal illustrations God gives them during a speech mean the most to people in the audience.

It is those moments of magic that may inspire the one person who will make the biggest impact in the world. Months or years later, someone will call a speaker's attention to something he said that created a turning point for the individual.

Speakers never quite get over how different that message was spoken than how it is heard by audience members. God is the Great Translator of our message when we speak truth. When we deliver a passionate and authentic message, people connect with us. When we dare to stand in front of an audience — any audience — we offer God the opportunity to use us and our words. It is indeed a huge risk. It is also a high calling.

Power Point 5: Your Message Positions You As an Authority

Craft the content of your message carefully because it helps you become the subject matter expert on your topic. Do everything you can to develop your experience and your expertise. Here are a few tips:

- Read every day on your topic of expertise. There is so much available information on the Internet in the form of blogs, video, and podcasts.
- Create your own experiments to gain more information in your field of expertise.
- Use your vocation and your passion as your live project.

Power Point 6: People Want You to Speak with Courage and Truth

You are powerful simply because of your position in the room as a speaker. Muster the courage to be vulnerable when you get the chance. Admit your mistakes willingly, and present them as an opportunity to teach others or build upon past lessons.

Are you a risk-adverse person? You aren't alone. Don't let the anxiety you feel steal your opportunity to experience life. The lessons you learn can allow others to learn through you.

Getting out of your comfort zone shows someone else that they too can get out of their comfort zone. If you don't, they might never either.

You may think you gain nothing except discomfort by taking a risk. The thing we often fear is the unknown. Knowing what to expect feels safer than stepping out to take a risk.

But what if that risk takes you to a better life? What if you make a mistake or fail at your attempt, but you learn a lesson that provides a stepping stone to something better?

And what if someone is watching you from a distance and your failed attempt teaches him something? What if that person sees that you took a risk, and it gave him the courage to take the same risk? What if he was more successful and made the world a better place because he was inspired by your courage?

It would indeed have been a sadder world if he saw that you were unwilling to take a risk, and so he thought he shouldn't either. We often don't realize we mentor people simply through our example. You may never become fearless, but I beg you to become a risk taker and chase life with reckless abandon.

Power Point 7: Everyone in Your Audience Listens Differently

There are three types of learners/communicators in an audience: visual, kinesthetic, and auditory.

Visual learners/communicators tend to sit in the back of the room. They want to take in the whole experience that includes not only what is happening on stage, but also in the audience.

The kinesthetic individuals sit on the front row. They learn by touch and feel and want to be close enough to be part of the experience.

The auditory person listens for meaning in the emotion and inflection as well as the spoken word. These people choose where they sit based on how they prefer to listen, communicate, and learn. They usually have no idea why they sit where they do. But when you understand who they are, you can craft your message for their individual needs.

This is why this is the most important power point — the

microphone is a valuable tool. If you don't use the it, people might not hear the real meaning in your message.

You probably realize the people in the back of the room can't hear as well as those in the front. However, the visual person may prefer to sit on the back row regardless of whether she can hear well when she is seated there. The hum of a ceiling fan or an air conditioner that cuts on while you are speaking will certainly drown out your "teacher voice."

You may not feel comfortable using a microphone, but it shows respect for every person in the room when you do.

When you are speaking, the attention may be on you, but remember your message delivery isn't about you. It is about the audience. The reason you speak is to articulate your message in a manner that helps everyone understand your meaning.

When you don't tune in to the needs of your audience, they will tune you out. You become just another talking head. *Blah blah-blah blah blah-blah.* Our time is too limited and too valuable not to spend it making a difference in the lives of others.

Yes, I think it is sad that we regard anyone with a microphone as the leader in the room. A microphone has no power. Everyone is worthy of holding it and speaking into it. But when we refuse to use it, we are subconsciously telling others that our message isn't important enough to be heard.

Conversely, when we grab the microphone and speak into it, we signal that our message is important. It also says that we are courageous. It is every bit as important as standing tall when we speak, versus sitting down to simply talk.

I'm not a big fan of "faking it until you make it." Stepping up and grabbing the microphone to share your knowledge and experience and passion isn't faking it at all. Proficiency is all in the process — prepare, deliver, learn, repeat. Each attempt teaches you something new — about speaking and about what you are made of.

Power Point 8: How You Hold the Microphone Matters

Holding the microphone is simple: hold it still and close to your mouth. Resist the urge to talk with your hands as you might point with the microphone. Don't let it sag as you speak. If someone else is holding the microphone, stay as close to it as possible.

Your message and all its nuances deserve to be heard by everyone in the room. Even someone you are convinced isn't listening might be the one paying the most attention. You never know when that message you spoke into the microphone is heard by your next potential client, employer, or decision maker. Whether or not you have the courage to speak into the microphone could indeed determine your future.

Reach out, grab that microphone, and hold it close to your mouth. You may utter the most important words of your life, and you want to make sure everyone can hear.

17
Look the Part

I went back and forth on whether to write this chapter. I give a polite nod to the topic in Chapter 5: Make a Confident First Impression. I don't want people to think they can't be confident if they aren't what the media defines as handsome or beautiful and thin.

However, there is a physical element to confidence. I'm convinced that the clothes you choose, your posture and stance, diet, and level of fitness play an important part in how you feel on the inside.

I've spent enough time photographing people who posed for publicity photos to study who is photogenic and why.

I worked for a company magazine and shooting publicity photos was an occasional part of my job. I always spent the time needed to get a good shot that would show the subjects in their best light. These shots would often end up in national industry magazines as well as our company publications.

A gorgeous young woman would come into the studio and

sit down. No matter what I did, I would struggle to get a natural, happy photo. It happened frequently with the most attractive of my subjects. The ones who worked the hardest on their appearance and person style were hardly ever what I would call photogenic.

Even though they were beautiful, they never relaxed behind the camera. Their smiles were forced and their eyes never had that glimmer. They almost always commented that they took terrible photos and hated having their picture taken. It took many more shots to get a photo that was nearly as attractive as the live person. And they hardly ever liked their photos when I did.

In contrast, I'd have an occasional subject come in who was almost homely. They came in all shapes and sizes but were generally not what you would consider attractive. But from the moment they walked in the door, they lit up the room.

They may not have had perfect teeth or skin or hair, but they had a warm, relaxed expression with happy eyes. The photo session nearly always moved quickly, and I had more great shots than they would ever need. They were far more likely to be photogenic than the most beautiful people.

What I discovered over the years was that being photogenic had little to do with being attractive. What was going on inside their head had far more impact than their outside appearance. I learned that people could smile with their eyes. In fact, the best expressions featured a sparkle in their eye and a partial smile. It looked authentic and natural.

I could tell who was confident and who was not from the moment they walked into the room for their photo session. The confident people carried themselves differently — they had a cheerful gate, stood tall, and leaned toward you when they spoke to you.

They took the experience in as a break from the usual routine of their business day. They enjoyed meeting someone new. They always thanked me for my time. I could tell who was advancing in their career quickly and who was not after just a few minutes behind the camera.

Looking the part definitely makes a difference. However, looking the part has little to do with being beautiful, handsome, or thin. You can look the part with the right clothing, fitness, diet, posture, and stance.

The Right Clothing

Dress in a way that makes you feel comfortable and well-appointed. It is wise to purchase fewer items and choose apparel that is classic and moves from day to evening and business to casual. Spend a little more if you can, but it isn't necessary. Because classic items don't go out of style, you can justify spending a little more to purchase something that will look good for hundreds of wearings.

Think carefully about where you most often go and buy appropriate clothing. If you use a company workout facility, make sure you wear good workout gear that flatters you and doesn't show too much skin. If you have casual Friday at your workplace, make sure you look professional enough to greet the president of the company should she or he walk into your office. When you dine out with friends, family, or coworkers, dress for an evening outing (not an evening on the couch). You don't need a lot of clothes, but make sure you have clothing that makes you feel good for any place you go.

Consider your body type when choosing apparel. The most expensive items will look cheap when they don't flatter the shape of your body. Choose items that won't go out of style quickly. Balance those with up-to-date, less-expensive shirts or accessories that will keep you looking current.

Shoes are an important part of your look. Make sure they are clean and polished. Spend a little more on a good pair of dress shoes. They will last longer and prove to be more comfortable. You'll get many more well-put-together outfits with a quality, well-maintained pair of shoes.

Fashions cycle every few years. This is a funny saying but one that has served me well: "If you were old enough to wear it the first time it was in style, you are too old to wear it when it comes back in style." No matter what your age, consider whether your clothing is age appropriate.

Fitness, Diet, Posture, and Stance

These four elements of your appearance have a greater effect on your perceived confidence than you'd ever imagine.

If you want to boost your confidence quickly, work out three to five days a week for three weeks. You'll notice a big change that will encourage you to keep it up.

A balanced regimen of cardio and strength training improves your posture, muscle tone (enhancing your bone structure), and circulation. You will stand taller, walk with more swagger, have a healthy glow, and experience fewer aches and pains (my favorite benefit of all since I am no longer a spring chicken).

If you have trouble fitting in a substantial workout at the

gym, take breaks during the workday to walk around your office building. Learn some yoga and Pilates moves that you can run through in about five minutes when you first get up in the morning.

My husband and I are empty nesters. When our daughter left home, we turned her room into a home gym. I still enjoy going to an exercise class at the gym, but it is nice to exercise at home too.

My mention of diet isn't really a commentary about being thin. My focus is on eating healthy. When you can pull together two healthy meals a day, it gives you a good foundation for your health. You have a lot more flexibility with that third meal.

Everyone's chemistry is different. Some of us were meant to eat more vegetables and fruit while others were meant to eat more meat. Do a little reading on healthy eating and find an approach that works for you and provides you the nutrients you need.

Watch your intake of excessive fat, sugar, caffeine, salt, and alcohol as these can affect how you look, act, and react under pressure. Your body's reaction to food additives can severely undermine you efforts to build your confidence.

My food allergies have been an annoyance for me for many years. I was in my late thirties when my food allergies could no longer be ignored. They affected how I felt and how I looked. The added inflammation and allergic reaction that results when you eat foods you shouldn't manifests itself as puffy eyes and mucus membranes, runny noses, puffy and uncomfortable digestive tracts, fatigue, and more unmentionable yuckiness. When you are dealing with a food allergy or sensitivity, your body is in crisis. It is in a weakened state, and you are more susceptible to illness. It is difficult to feel confident when you don't feel well.

Fitness and diet have a great affect on your posture and stance. A little preparation can go a long way in sending the right message to those you meet. Regardless of how handsome or beautiful you are or you body type , you can easily be the most attractive, confident person in the room by following these tips.

18
Give It All to God

Two days before this book went to print, I was working in the early morning hours on the cover. I followed my usual process in Adobe Illustrator, the software I use for creating book covers and other artwork.

I was playing with different layouts. I sampled several colors, fonts, and effects. Type is the most important element of the front cover. The idea is to make the type as large as possible because many book images on the Internet are displayed so small.

I was using the template from another book I published a couple years earlier. It saves me time to reuse some elements of the layout. It was from a book titled *I Still Need a Father*. I moved the elements I wasn't reusing over to the side of the screen — mostly text from the previous cover.

I eventually settled on a design. I moved all the unused type over to the side, just in case I changed my mind.

It wasn't until the next day that I noticed a message in the collage of text next to my cover design. There it was, "Father, I Still Need You."

Just One More Chapter

For days, I felt like there was one more chapter I needed to include in this book. I've struggled the last three days to write it. The words and ideas just wouldn't mesh. Even with my best writer's-block-busting technique, I couldn't put it together. I would work on something else for awhile and then take another run at it. Nothing.

Now that I've had a few hours to process the meaning of the collage, the words for this final chapter are flowing. The book interior and cover art are both ready to send to the printer, but this chapter beckons to be included. It isn't the same topic I thought this additional chapter would cover. This one is the perfect addition though.

We Need Him No Matter How Successful We Become

The message in the collage is crystal clear: no matter how confident we become in our abilities, we still need God beside us every step of the way. Bam!

God knows us so well. When we become more capable of accomplishing tasks on our own, we stop relying on Him. That is dangerous territory. We must remember that He cares about our development and our success, and He wants to walk with us. He wants us to come to Him with our questions and talk with Him before we make decisions. He wants to use our efforts to do His work on Earth. He cares as much about the smallest details of our lives as he does our mighty missions. We are more successful when we include God in every part of our lives. Our success is borrowed. It belongs to God.

The Journey Finally Comes to an End

I fast a couple times a year. I do it for health reasons mostly, but it is a great time to connect with God and reach out to Him with more intention. When you fast, your body doesn't have the mental resources to multi-task. I enjoy this time of mental peace and the ability to focus. When I'm not juggling a dozen thoughts in my head, I have an easier time hearing that still, quiet voice.

The content for a book on confidence had been on my heart for awhile. I'm not sure whether it was a calling or just a desire of my heart. I had published many books for others authors before and after I wrote my last book in 2008. It was time for me to commit my latest book to paper. Life was busy though. Most people lack the discipline to take on the time and mental commitment of the process.

I started a ten-day fast right before my birthday in March 2013. I brainstormed the content and the title for this book on my birthday. No temporary working title for me. I bought the website domain name the same day. I even made a folder for it. This was going to happen.

I can always tell when I'm working on a God-led project, because life gets in the way — in epic proportion. A few life events stole my attention. We were working on a large-scale home renovation, I joined a band, I ran for public office, a pipe froze and broke over our living room, and my dad died. I'm probably forgetting a few items; but yeah, life got in the way.

When I sat down to write my 2015 goals, I carried over the goal to write the confidence book — again. One July morning, I scratched off "Write and publish confidence book" from my list of goals. My heart sank, but it just didn't feel like a project I could tackle in 2015. I moved on.

In December of 2015, I was finishing up a long list of volunteer responsibilities. It had been an exhausting year, and I had just announced that I would run for mayor of my city in 2016. Our home renovation was nearing completion, and I was deeply involved it. Clearly, I had many things on my mind. Thank goodness I wasn't beating myself up about not writing that confidence book. There would be other years — probably not 2016 as that mayor campaign would take all my extra time. Other years.

Around the middle of December, I was planing what I would teach at a book-writing retreat the coming January. I thought about that confidence book again and sighed. How many people at that retreat would attend in preparation for writing their books and speeches to share their messages and life experiences? How many never would accomplish it because life got in the way? I should be setting the example! I should be demonstrating how we can overcome challenges of answering a calling. I was bummed that I had let life get in the way of publishing my confidence book for yet another year, but I gave it to God.

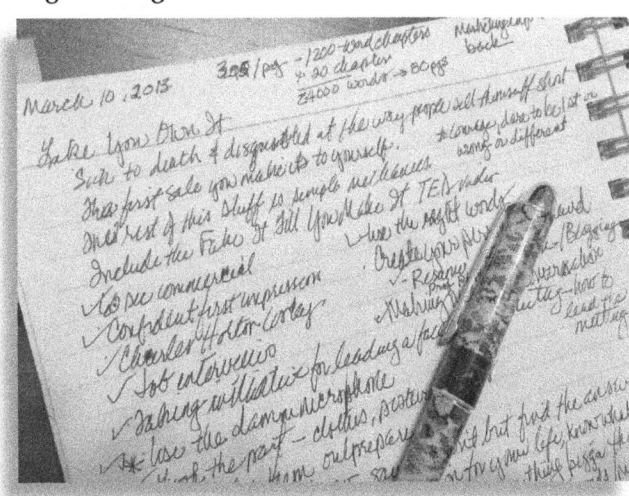

In a few days, I was filled with new questions about my book. It was originally designed to consist of less than twenty chapters, all around 1,200 words. I could do that, couldn't I? I'm a book editor, designer, and publisher. Surely, I could write a chapter an hour. The information was all in my head. Some of the story ideas for the chapters were inspired by experiences that happened earlier in the month.

That night was the first in a string of 2:00 a.m. awakenings and nights I couldn't sleep when I did go to bed. Each time, I sat down to type, the words came easily. Brainstorming the list of topics for the book more than two years earlier provided me a flexible structure. It allowed me to jump around to whatever technique I was on fire for that day. Thank goodness personal development nonfiction doesn't have to flow in chronological order.

And that is pretty much how it happened, except that a chapter took at least two hours to write. Go figure that I would underestimate something like that. The process of editing, layout, and cover design went smoothly too. I would never have chosen those three weeks to write, design, and publish a book; but God chose them for me.

When we ask for His guidance and invite Him to be part of every single feat we attempt, He shows up big. Before we walk into a room of new people, He is there with us. When we give a presentation or run a meeting, He is there. He wants us to ask him for guidance before we make decisions or launch new ventures. He wants us to succeed, and He wants to catch us when we stumble. God has our back. We just have to involve Him in the process.

Nothing Happens by Accident

Just as I committed the outline of this project to God, and He provided me with the discipline to nail my tail to a chair when I had a perfectly undistracted window of time. I am grateful He gave me this final message to add: Father, I Still Need You.

So this chapter wasn't on the original plan from March 2013, but here it is. The purpose of this chapter is to remind you that no matter how confident in your abilities you become, they come from God, and He wants to be included in everything you attempt. Yes, God, we still need You.

I'm giving it all to you, God, like You own it — because You do. I'm overwhelmed by what you continue to do through my efforts. Wow! Thank you.

19
Soar

Here is how the process I've given you looks the next time you enter a room:
Before you walk into a room or a meeting, take a moment to stop and breathe deeply (you'd be surprised how shallow your breathing is when you are nervous). Straighten your clothes and throw your shoulders back. Allow your arms to hang comfortably next to your body.

Don't worry about your appearance. You look great. Besides, no one cares and isn't paying any attention. You've done your homework, and you are ready to work the room like you own it.

As you approach someone, smile and greet him. Lean forward as you reach to shake hands. Follow the Meaningful Conversation Template from Chapter 12. You've got this. Brace yourself for a great, confident future.

Go get 'em, tiger! Rawrrr!

Book Carrie for Your Next Meeting or Conference

Carrie Perrien Smith MBA is a training, communication, and publishing industry veteran. She ran screaming from her corporate career in 2001. Even though she sometimes misses regular paychecks, a cubicle with office supplies she didn't have to purchase, and normal working hours, she wouldn't trade the entrepreneur's kill-what-you-eat lifestyle (most days, at least).

Today, this third-generation entrepreneur runs a marketing, branding, and publishing company. She works internationally with business leaders, candidates, and growing companies who want to brand themselves as experts in their industry and build a speaking and consulting business.

Business owners trust Carrie because she's one of them. She's the first one in line to mentor them, challenge their ideas, cheer them on, and sometimes catch them before they go over the cliff. She supports causes that pave the way for business owners because they are the foundation and the future of our economy.

Carrie mingles the best of the old-school, tried-and-true techniques with new-tech publishing and communication tools to help her clients build a brand that screams EXPERT AND WORTH EVERY PENNY!

She most enjoys working with emerging leaders and business owners. A grateful woman of faith, Carrie uses her life's work and volunteer service to honor and serve God. She devotes hundreds of hours each year to her community.

She started her company, Soar with Eagles, in 2003. Also a speaker, consultant, and writer, Carrie is the author of *Currency: Striking Networking Gold in a Relationship Economy*. She writes a blog for *NWAMotherlode.com* called *Empty Nexter* and has hosted an Internet radio show called *Business: Engaged!* She and her husband publish their blog *HouseoftheBlackDogs.com* where they talk about paws, love, and rock and roll.

Carrie holds a Bachelor of Science in Organizational Management and a Masters in Business Administration with an emphasis in Leadership and Ethics, both from John Brown University.

She lives in Rogers, Arkansas with her husband Tom. They are in a classic rock party band called Paper Jam. They share their empty nest with their rescued and now hopelessly spoiled fur children Jazmin with Teeth, Midgieboy, and Chloe Needletoes.

If you can't find Carrie on the Internet, you haven't tried. But in case you need some clues, you can follow her on Twitter @soarwitheagles or @businessengaged or connect with her on Facebook and LinkedIn. You'll find her making her community a better place on Twitter and Instagram at @carrie4rogers.

Another Book by Carrie Perrien Smith

Currency: Striking Networking Gold in a Relationship Economy

**More Clients.
Bigger Paydays.
Sweeter Success.**

We live in a relationship economy. WHO you know is every bit as important as WHAT you know. In *Currency*, Carrie Perrien Smith shares the secret to garnering the respect you deserve. It's nice to have friends, but it's priceless to have fans who rave about you to others. These are the people who can connect you to mentors, clients, and next steps in your career. *Currency: Striking Networking Gold in a Relationship Economy* provides tools that will enable you to:

- Build a solid business referral network using shameless self-promotion.

- Use word power to position yourself as someone who is influential, engaging, and in high demand.
- Deliver an unforgettable customer experience that will boost your bottom line.
- Build a lasting brand that grows in value and leaves a legacy.

You can order additional copies of both books at online book stores and at www.**LikeYouOwnIt**.com.

Quantity discounts are available by contacting Soar with Eagles (www.soarhigher.com).

Buy It for Someone You Believe In

Purchase *Like You Own It* as a gift or self-development resource for family members, friends, and team members.

www.ingramcontent.com/pod-product-compliance
Lightning Source LLC
Chambersburg PA
CBHW060017050426
42448CB00012B/2791